Loyalty

Those Who ARE PROUD

DAG HEWARD-MILLS

Parchment House

Unless otherwise stated, all Scripture quotations are taken from the King James Version of the Bible.

THOSE WHO ARE PROUD

Originally published by Parchment House 2013
under the title
FORMULA FOR HUMILITY
15th Printing 2017

Copyright © 2017 Dag Heward-Mills

First published 2017 by Parchment House
2nd Printing 2018

Find out more about Dag Heward-Mills at:

Healing Jesus Campaign
Write to: evangelist@daghewardmills.org
Website: www.daghewardmills.org
Facebook: Dag Heward-Mills
Twitter: @EvangelistDag

ISBN : 978-1-68398-269-2

Dedication

I dedicate this book to my friend, *Reverend Steve Mensah.*
Thank you for many years of good friendship and fellowship.
Thank you for your awesome message on humility that inspired this teaching.

All rights reserved under international copyright law. Written permission must be secured from the publisher to use or reproduce any part of this book.

Contents

Introduction: Those Who Are Proud v

1. Humble Yourself 1
2. How To Be Humble Like a Child 8
3. How To Be Humble Like a Servant 25
4. Mind Not High Things 37
5. How To Diagnose "Proud Speaking" 42
6. What it Means To Have A Proud Look 62
7. Humble Yourself Means "Do it yourself" 67
8. What it Means To Be A Humble Minister Like Jesus Christ 72
9. What It Means To Be Puffed Up 80
10. What It Means To Be Puffed Up Like Lucifer 83
11. What It Means To Be Puffed Up Like Vashti 89
12. What It Means To Be Puffed Up Like Nebuchadnezzar 94
13. What It Means To Be Puffed Up Like Belshazzar 100
14. What It Means To Be Puffed Up Like Rehoboam 104
15. What It Means To Be Puffed Up Like Pharaoh 109
16. What It Means To Be Puffed Up Like Korah 113
17. What Is It Like To Fall From Pride? 117

Introduction: Those Who Are Proud

Pride is the most deadly evil that afflicts the human race. It is an invisible evil that has started more quarrels and more wars than you could ever imagine. Pride is the reason for the conflicts and the confusion in our world. We are desperately in need of a formula for humility that will deliver us from "those who are proud."

> **Only by pride cometh contention: but with the well advised is wisdom.**
>
> Proverbs 13:10

Since the serpent took a "bite" of the human race, this deadly poison has been running in our veins. Pride is a universal, spiritual and pervasive evil. It is difficult to find any part of our world that does not have proud people. People do not have to own anything to be proud. People just have to exist on this earth and they will become proud for some reason. The history of our world is a history of wars and conflicts. The history of war is the history of the manifestation of pride. Human history is the history of satanic nature working itself out through man.

All marital problems and conflicts are caused by pride. Satan is the father of anyone who manifests in pride. Satan is the one who inspires pride, arrogance and conflict. The bitter fights that take place between husbands and wives are caused by pride. All who walk in pride are walking under the influence of satan.

...He (satan) is a king over all the children of pride.
Job 41:34

In church today, all our problems are caused by pride. We badly need a formula for humility. All the conflicts in churches, between pastors, their assistants and other leaders, are caused by pride. All the disloyalty, treachery and breakaways in churches are caused by people who think they are as good as the leader. They are great in their own eyes and see no reason why they should be under someone's leadership. They say to themselves, "Why should a great person like me stay under someone like you? I am also as good as you are!"

The disloyalty of the people you lead is caused by the pride in them. Satan inspires them to do what he did when he was in heaven. When Lucifer was in heaven, he dwelt in glory and he had a very high rank.

One day, he said to himself, "Why should I stay at this level when I could be even higher?" He said to himself, "I will take my leadership gift to its logical conclusion. I will arise and displace the One who sits on the throne. I will replace Almighty God on His throne. I will be just like the Most High."

Satan was so full of self-importance and self-conceit that he rebelled against the One who created and appointed him. Many angels believed the delusions and joined in the rebellion against their creator. Today, many ministers and associate ministers have the same kind of thinking. They are filled with delusions of who they are. Unfortunately, it takes time for delusions to unravel themselves.

Delusions take about ten years to completely unravel and destroy those who believe them. A very strong delusion and deception may continue undetected for five years. But after that, the evidence of the deception begins to come out. Adolf Hitler began to lead Germany into damnation when he took power in 1933. By 1939, it began to be evident that he was a criminal seeking to destroy the world. Adolf Hitler began the Second World War in 1939. By 1942, after the defeat of the German army at Stalingrad, it was clear to many Germans that they had believed a lie. The war and the conquest were based on a delusion that Adolf Hitler was the perfect leader with the perfect solutions for this world. The war was based on the delusion that Jews were the cause of all the problems in the world. By 1945, Adolf Hitler had systematically murdered six million Jews and everyone knew that Germany had been led by a mentally deranged mass murderer. As you can see, it took about ten years for the delusions to completely unravel themselves. When you follow a rebellious and disloyal pastor, it will take about ten years for you to realize that you have followed a mistake.

Many ministers are destroyed when they follow delusions. They may not be following a crazed Jew-hater like Adolf Hitler but they are following a delusion when they follow a rebellion. As I said, it takes time for delusions to be completely unravelled and for pastors to see the mistakes they have made.

It is important to understand our invisible enemy called pride. You may defeat all enemies but pride may be standing strong by your side. Why is that? Pride is invisible and that is why it escapes notice! Through this book, you will receive a special understanding that will help you defeat an invisible enemy. You will be delivered from unwittingly joining "those who are proud."

The aim of this book is to make pride "visible and identifiable!!"

The aim of this book is to make humility attainable!!

The aim of this book is to deliver you from the ranks of "those who are proud."

Humble yourself by the side of the Lord and He will lift you up! What a blessing it is to be lifted up by the Lord! Every spiritual warrior would love to destroy this invisible enemy. The last enemy in the battle is the invisible, intangible dragon of pride! "Those who are proud" are the captives of this invisible dragon. This book gives you the strategy to uncover the dragon and drive it out of your midst.

This enemy called "Pride" has escaped destruction by being invisible. Through this book you will see through the delusions that make us all so proud. Through the revelation of being a "child "or being a "servant", you will have a practical key in your hand to unlock the rivers and blessings of humility for your life!

Jesus said, "the greatest" in the Kingdom will be the most humble. This is why satan strives so hard to position you amongst "those who are proud". Once you are amongst "those who are proud" it means you will be amongst the least in heaven. This book grants you a divine escape from being among the least in heaven. This book grants you a divine escape from "those who are proud". Enjoy the formula for humility that delivers you from the group called "Those Who Are Proud."

CHAPTER 1

Humble Yourself

Humble yourselves in the sight of the Lord, and he shall lift you up.

James 4:10

People define pride in many different ways. People may say you are proud because you are a quiet person. People may say you are proud because you are tall and confident. People may say you are proud because you drive a nice, shiny air-conditioned car.

So what really is pride? Does it matter whether you are humble or proud?

Indeed it does matter! We must humble ourselves before the Lord. We must live in a way that God considers to be humble.

The instruction is clear! *Humble yourself in the sight of the Lord* and not in the sight of man. There is no point in practicing a brand of humility that God does not accept. Humility is a virtue defined and described by God Himself. Human beings define humility in many different ways but God's definition of humility is what matters to us.

Humility is so important that it is worth searching the length and breadth of the scriptures until we know for sure what it is. The warnings about pride are too frightening to ignore.

In this first chapter, I want us to look at the reasons why we should humble ourselves before the Lord.

Seven Reasons Why You Should Humble Yourself

1. Humble yourself because God resists proud people.

> But he giveth more grace. Wherefore he saith, GOD RESISTETH THE PROUD, but giveth grace unto the humble.
>
> James 4:6

Pride is so contrary to God that He has declared war on all who are proud. When you become proud, God will become your enemy and oppose you in all that you do.

People who have become proud, often do not realise that God has began to oppose them. Sometimes Christians rebuke the devil because they think satan is the one fighting them. But where it concerns proud Christians, the devil can go on a holiday. God Himself takes over and opposes the proud.

You may even find yourself rebuking God because He is opposing you and your pride. I wouldn't like to rebuke God, would you? I wouldn't like God to be my enemy. Would you like God to be your enemy? God is the only one who loves you the way you are. If He also becomes your enemy, what is left of you?

2. **Humble yourself because God gives grace to humble people.**

    But he giveth more grace. Wherefore he saith, GOD resisteth the proud, but GIVETH GRACE UNTO THE HUMBLE.

    James 4:6

Amazingly, God gives undeserved help to humble people. Grace is undeserved help and favour. When you lower yourself, God reacts by sending you grace. How nice it must be to receive undeserved help when you take the humble path of humility! Perhaps, there is no better reason to humble yourself than this. Think about all the undeserved help you could have in your life and ministry if you were to humble yourself.

Do you want God to give undeserved help to your church? Do you want God to give you undeserved help in your pastoral ministry? Then humble yourself! Do you want God to give you undeserved help in your evangelistic ministry? Then humble yourself!

Do you want God to give you underserved help in your finances? Then humble yourself! Do you want God to help you in your moral life? Then humble yourself! Do you want God to give you a lot of help so that you can be holy? Then humble yourself! Almost every spiritual activity is aided by humility.

When you humble yourself supernatural grace is given to you. Try it and see. Be humble! Be like a child and a servant and see if changes do not begin to appear in your life.

What about your marriage? Do you want God to help you in your difficult relationship? Humbling yourself is the key to receiving the undeserved help that you need.

3. **Humble yourself because through that you will be lifted up to the next level in life.**

> Humble yourselves in the sight of the Lord, and HE SHALL LIFT YOU UP.
>
> James 4:10

The next important reason for you to be humble is for promotion. Who doesn't want to be lifted up and promoted? The lifting of the Lord and the exaltation of the Lord are the gifts you receive for being humble. Notice the scripture clearly. When you go down, God will lift you up.

Are you not seeking for increase and promotion? Then humble yourself and be a servant! Humble yourself and become a child who can be trained and instructed.

You will find yourself rising out of your current level into heights you never dreamed of.

> Humble yourselves therefore under the mighty hand of God, that HE MAY EXALT YOU IN DUE TIME
>
> 1 Peter 5:6

Think about it. What does it mean to be exalted? Exaltation is to be gloriously lifted up into beauty and shining excellence. Is that not what you want? Humility is the key to enter these realms.

4. **Humble yourself so that you will be covered and protected.**

> Likewise, ye younger, submit yourselves unto the elder. Yea, all of you be subject one to another, and BE

CLOTHED WITH HUMILITY: for God resisteth the proud, and giveth grace to the humble.

1 Peter 5:5

Humility is a spiritual covering. Humility is not just an attitude. Humility is not just a poor and simple way of living. Humility is not the art of looking timid and defeated. Humility is actually a spiritual cloak that covers you. It protects the Christian from many unseen and spiritually disastrous evils. Put on humility and you will be covered, delivered and protected from many evils in this life.

5. **Humble yourself because your pride is the signal for your soon-to-come destruction, your fall and your shame.**

A MAN'S PRIDE SHALL BRING HIM LOW: but honour shall uphold the humble in spirit.

Proverbs 29:23

PRIDE GOETH BEFORE DESTRUCTION, and an haughty spirit before a fall.

Proverbs 16:18

WHEN PRIDE COMETH, THEN COMETH SHAME: but with the lowly is wisdom.

Proverbs 11:2

Pride is a signal! It signals a coming fall, a coming catastrophe and a coming evil. Humbling yourself will remove the looming dangers from your life and ministry. Satan is greatly attracted to your self-exaltation and over confident utterances. They are an open door to him.

Pride is a spiritual signal that assembles demons of shame, destruction and defeat. Your pride is like a trumpet that gives a sure and definite call to evil spirits.

When you are proud, angels are not called in to help you. When you are proud, demons are assembled to destroy you. You are actually more accessible to demons because your spiritual clothing and covering are removed.

6. **Humble yourself in the sight of the Lord because pride is essentially satanic and demonic.**

> Canst thou draw out leviathan with an hook? Or his tongue with a cord which thou lettest down? Canst thou put an hook into his nose?..
>
> He beholdeth all high things: HE IS A KING OVER ALL THE CHILDREN OF PRIDE.
>
> Job 41:1, 34

All proud people have a king and that king is satan. Satan is the king of all the children of pride. You must decide to humble yourself so that satan will not be your king and ruler. Once you walk in pride you live and walk under the rulership of satan himself.

Pride is essentially demonic and satanic. Satan fell out of heaven through his presumption, arrogance and pride. In pride he lifted himself up against God! Lucifer exalted himself against the throne of God and threatened to ascend to replace God in His throne. This was the most outrageous manifestation of pride ever.

But God cast satan out of heaven and showed him that he was nothing but a rebellious branch, puffed up and swelled up for no reason. This evil puffing up and swelling up is what affects the entire human race. Human beings feel so big and great without having any good reason to. Today, large sections of the human race foolishly say that there is no God.

Unfortunately, we the ministers of the gospel also become swollen when we achieve little bitty goals in the ministry. Most pride has no foundation. Pride is mostly idiopathic (without a known cause). Ministers of the gospel swell up and attack their spiritual fathers who raised them up. Associates swell up and attempt to ascend into the chair of the leader. Soldiers rise up and attempt to remove legitimately elected heads of state. These things happen because people swell up and see themselves as bigger than they really are.

The words "pride" and "satan" are virtually synonymous. Satan is a spirit! But pride is the attitude and speech that is caused by the presence of satan!

Anytime you see pride in an individual, you are recognising the presence of a very evil spirit – satan! Satan is the originator of pride. That is why God hates pride and opposes anyone in whom He detects this pride!

7. Humble yourself in the sight of the Lord because your pride will make you an abomination to God.

Every one that is proud in heart IS AN ABOMINATION to the Lord: though hand join in hand, he shall not be unpunished.

Proverbs 16:5

God does not only resist the proud, but the proud are an abomination to Him.

This scripture means that God is outraged at proud people. He loathes stubborn people. It is not a good thing for God to detest and dislike you. I suggest that you turn away from everything that is associated with pride so that God will not be filled with revulsion when He thinks of you.

CHAPTER 2

How To Be Humble Like a Child

Except ye be converted, and BECOME AS LITTLE CHILDREN,

Matthew 18:3

LET HIM BE AS THE YOUNGER . . .

Luke 22:26

What is the formula for humility? How can we acquire this vague spiritual virtue? Because pride is a nebulous and vague evil, it is easily disguised and comes to us in many forms. It is no surprise that most people who claim to be humble are actually proud. It is also no surprise that many things that are called humility are actually not humility. For instance, people who speak with an unusual accent are sometimes thought of as proud. Rich people, prominent people and confident people are also wrongly accused of being proud. But many of these people are not actually proud.

So how can we know when someone is actually humble or proud? Jesus Christ the Son of God came to this world to show us *the way* to humility, *the truth* about humility and *the life* of humility. His simple formula for humility is what this book is about.

The answer to pride is simple – be a child or be a servant! Jesus said, "Whosoever therefore shall humble himself as this little child …". This is important because Jesus is telling us that a child is humble. I would not have thought of a child as being humble or having any virtues.

I would have thought of a child as being infantile, naïve, basic or even stupid! But Jesus described the behaviour of a child as humility. It is therefore important for us to study the characteristics of a child and accept them as real humility.

How can you be humble? How can you humble yourself? Truly, Jesus gave us the formula for humility when He said, "Whosoever therefore shall humble himself as this little child, the same is greatest in the kingdom of heaven" (Matthew 18:4). Humility is the most important virtue for Christians because it is what makes you great in the kingdom. Who wouldn't want to be great in the kingdom of God? If you want to be great in the kingdom, study all you can about humility and put it into action. With all your might strive to become like a child. The more childlike you are the more humble you are!

What It Means To Be Humble Like A Child

1. **When you are humble like a child, you quickly forgive and forget. When you lose this humility, you no longer forgive and forget.**

    Most adults do not forgive easily. Children have a short attention span and a short memory. It takes humility to let go of issues. As you get older and prouder, you know what is right and you know when people are behaving wrongly. As you get older, you become more conscious of when you are being cheated and when you are getting the bad end of the stick. Because of that, an older and prouder person does not easily give up issues or forget the wrongs that have been done to him. You would like to prove the point and show people how people how badly they have behaved.

    This righteous anger is actually a manifestation of our pride. Children, on the other hand, have quarrels as they play together but will be found playing happily together a few minutes after the quarrel. A grown-up will carry on with the quarrel and decide not to speak, smile or flow around any more. How different grown-ups are from children!

    To be humble therefore, is to *not* continue to quarrel. To be humble is to decide *not* to remain unhappy with your fellow brother or sister. Pastors display great pride by having conflicts with each other, not flowing with each other and fighting one another from the pulpit.

    When a man finds a beautiful young lady who respects and honours him, he marries her knowing that he has found a humble, submissive creature whom he can lead about for the rest of his life.

    Unfortunately, the humility and submissive nature which attracted the man soon fades away. Soon, the prouder and more confident wife comes into conflict with an equally proud and confident husband. The clashes begin and both parties feel they are right. Everyone feels cheated and disappointed. "I will never forget, I will never forgive" are the unspoken promises that spouses make to each other after their marital clashes.

When the couple were in a relationship and there was a lot of humility, nothing was able to stir up such quarrels. With pride came quarrels. "Only by pride cometh contention..." (Proverbs 13:10). Because of the increase in pride in couples, there is more contention, more unforgiveness and more divorce. Indeed, without humility you cannot enter the kingdom's blessing of permanent love and marriage.

2. **When you are humble like a child, you sit quietly and listen to instructions and teachings. When you lose this humility, you no longer sit quietly and listen to instructions, teachings and guidance.**

When you are humble like a child, you allow yourself to be led. You are guidable, malleable and "leadable". When you lose this humility, you do not want to be led or taught by anyone. You want to be independent. Your pride makes you stiff and independent. You take great pride in claiming independence.

Children sit quietly and receive instructions in the classroom. Grown-ups are able to gather them into groups and teach them. When people are filled with pride, they resent being put in a group. They resent having to be a part of little groups that are being taught.

"I am not a small boy," they say in their hearts. "I do not see why I should attend that meeting. Who is that bible study leader and why should I listen to his ideas?" You rarely find rich proud people attending small group meetings. These people rarely attend prayer meetings, bible studies or Sunday School meetings. They are too big and too proud to sit still and be taught the word of God. Perhaps, such people would be more comfortable in a large Sunday service of a prominent cathedral in their city.

But remember that when you were a child you were gathered into little groups and taught songs, poems and hymns. Remember that when you were humble you could attend services and receive teachings and blessings. If you want to be humble, decide to be like a child. Decide to join the groups. Decide to be someone who can be gathered and organised alongside with others. Decide to be someone who can be taught and trained in new things. What a blessing will come over you as you walk in humility!

3. **When you are humble like a child, you easily learn new things. When you lose this humility, you do not easily learn anything new.**

Learning new things is another sign that you still have some humility around you. When we become proud we are unable to read books and learn the new things God wants to bring us into. Ministers of the gospel stop learning at the rate at which they become proud. Unable to receive from people they despise, they stop growing in the Lord and they stop growing in the ministry. Many ministries have come to a plateau because of their inability to learn new things and to find new ways of doing old things.

But the real problem is not that you cannot learn new things. The real problem is that pride has taken away childlikeness from you and prevented you from being capable of learning anything new. Unfortunately, God often brings new things for us to learn through vessels we least expect.

It may be someone from a different country, different tribe or different colour. He may have a funny accent or he may be too young for you to receive from him. He may be someone you consider to be inferior. Because of this, you are forced to stop learning and to remain the size that you grew to when you were humble. Church growth would have happened in your ministry if you could have learnt something new.

You would have entered into a miracle ministry if you could have learnt some new things. Humility would have made you into a child and given you the ability to become a better musician and a better singer in the kingdom.

We all grow up and knowing certain things. Without humility you will not be able to learn the many more new things that you need to know for your ministry. Pride indeed keeps you in a state of a permanent fall.

4. When you are humble like a child, you copy things easily. When you lose this humility, you do not want to copy, even if it is a good thing.

There are many methods of learning. Copying is the divine method given to children to make them surge forward and catch up with adults. Children copy easily and that is why they are able to learn languages quickly. Grown-ups are filled with pride and are unable to copy something successful from their neighbour. It takes great humility to copy someone. When people copy, they try to hide the fact that they learnt something from you.

Here are the words of the proud one who cannot and will not copy. He says: "I want to be an original! I am not a copy of anyone! I didn't copy what I know! I learnt it by myself! I am an original! God revealed it to me Himself from heaven!" How nice it sounds to be able to say that everything about you is original.

In my ministry, I have found the art of copying to be the key to surging forward and catching up with people I look up to. In other words, humility is the key to surging forward and catching up with those ahead of you.

I have been able to surge forward into the ministry of teaching and preaching by copying Fred Price. I have been able to surge forward into church growth by copying Yonggi Cho. I have been able to surge forward into the ministry of miracles by copying Benny Hinn. I have been able to surge forward into the mass crusades in Africa by copying Reinhard Bonnke.

I have a very long list of things that I have copied from others. I have no shame about this. I am glad I copied them. It has changed my life! It has changed my ministry! It has changed everything about me! When you are too big to copy you will stay down.

So what about you? When are you going to start copying good

things so that you can surge forward and catch up with those who have left you so far behind? When are you going to lay aside your pride and become a little child again? O for another chance at greatness through the key of humility!

5. **When you are humble like a child, you are not conscious of the wealth of others. When you lose this humility, you relate to people based on their wealth.**

Little children are not conscious of wealth or riches. The son of a millionaire will play games with the child from the slums without thinking about who they are. It is when the simplicity and humility of childlikeness departs from you that you become conscious of what people have. It is your pride that makes you find out where people live, what car they drive and how much money they have. The humble eyes of a child do not notice these things.

When you become humble you will no longer notice or look out for the symbols of wealth. You will no longer relate to people according to how much money they have or where they live. This is the reason why many people cannot be in the ministry. They do not want to relate to the poor and the down-and-outers of the society. But our Christian religion forces us to be humble and to relate with the sick, poor, handicapped and the lame. Pride therefore keeps you away from true ministry because it keeps you away from the poor.

When you have the humility of a child, you will be able to receive the right husband or the right woman for your life. A good wife or husband may not have so much money to show. If all you are doing is looking at the wealth of your potential partner, your pride will lead you to a fall.

When pastors' eyes are filled with pride, they look for wealth in their members. They visit wealthy people and go for exquisite dinners with the prominent members of their church. They hardly visit the young or the poor members because they have no money to offer. Your pride has led you away from the humble sheep that need your help most. You need humble eyes to be a good minister of the gospel.

6. **When you are humble like a child, you are not conscious of people's nationalities. When you lose this humility, you become conscious of people's nationalities.**

Little children are not conscious of which country a person comes from. Neither are they conscious of a person's accent or colour. Grown-ups are very conscious of these things and will not allow their children to marry from certain countries or tribes. As you grow up and the evil of pride enters your soul, you become conscious of many things that a child never notices. National pride and tribal pride are evil spirits that enter into adults. Look carefully and you will see that there is nothing like that in children.

Through humility you will be able to marry someone from another country or tribe. Some people will remain unmarried because they did not have the humility to marry someone from another country. Some people will not receive spiritual blessings from white men because they belong to a black movement that looks down on white preachers.

God can give you great blessings through "white", "blue" and "yellow" pastors. Why have you become conscious of things that do not matter to God? You are filled with the spirit of pride. The humility you need is gone! You are in trouble because you have lost your humility.

7. **When you are humble like a child, you do not cover your natural weaknesses. When you lose this humility you always do your best to make a good impression.**

A humble person does not care about what people think about him. A humble person does not care whether you are impressed or not. The proud people of this world need to keep up appearances and impress the world. Children can bathe and stand naked by the side of the road without thinking much about it. When you lose your innocence and your humility you are unable to undress or bathe by the roadside. You are conscious of what you look like and what people think of you. Children do not worry about what people think about them. They are not concerned about what anybody thinks. They have no need to constantly impress others with a good outward show.

Pride in a woman is revealed by her constant need to look sharp, beautiful and impressive to the outside world. The need for make-up and special hair-dos is fuelled by the pride of life.

Many ladies do not present their real and normal selves to us. But at home they cover their hair, take off their necklaces and jewellery and become real. Outside, they are full of smiles and pleasantries that are unreal. Their need to stay up high on the scale and be impressive to the outside world reveals how far they are from being little children.

8. When you are humble like a child, you are trusting and believing.

Little children believe many fantastic stories such as the story of Santa Claus. I have enjoyed telling my children stories. Many times I sought and searched for stories so I could tell my children interesting stories. I have found myself enjoying the stories as much as they seemed to enjoy the stories. One day, my grown up sons heard my little daughter rehearsing a story I had told them and they asked, "Is Daddy still telling you those stories?? They had once enjoyed my stories but had grown too big for these same stories.

So it is with our spiritual lives. When we are humble like children, we believe many fantastic stories. We believe the bible. We believe all teachings. We believe in giving. We believe in tithing. We believe in miracles. We believe in signs and wonders.

When you are a child, you trust your father even though he may be an adulterer or an irresponsible man. As far as you are concerned, he is your father! So it is when you are humble like a child! You believe the man of God and trust what he says. People who have become proud, do not believe what pastors say anymore. They no longer believe the stories and messages of the man of God. Pride makes you sceptical of men of God. Pride makes you come up with excuses for not believing in anything any more.

When people are filled with pride they begin to criticise their own parents and rebuke them for not being worthy parents. When pride fills the eyes and the heart of a son, he finds fault with his father and speaks about his father's shortcomings. A prideful daughter will rebuke her own mother or father for not being a good enough provider.

Try sitting in church by a man filled with pride and arrogance. He will make negative comments about the pastor, the preaching and the church. He will reject the messenger and the message, reducing every argument to absurdity. You may reject the word of God, but it is not because you are knowledgeable or learned. It is because you are proud. Your negative comments about a preacher are not a sign of your being educated or wise. They are a sign of the evil pride of man which has filled your soul.

Man of God, it is time to humble yourself and receive people whom God has sent to you. It is time to believe the bible again and to receive the messages that are coming to you from the Holy Spirit. Become a child and believe in the vision and messages of the Holy Spirit to you. Remember, when you are humble you become great in the kingdom. Remember, when you are humble you will believe the fantastic visions, dreams and messages from God's servants to you.

9. **When you are humble like a child, you are not conscious of your living circumstances. When you lose this humility you become conscious of your circumstances.**

When you are a child, you are not conscious of your living circumstances. You are not even aware of which country you live in. When my children were smaller, they did not understand where exactly they were. I would take them to a town in the western part of Ghana but they never understood that they were still in Ghana. It did not matter to them. Everywhere was good enough, once their parents were there.

Pride leads people to live in certain places even though it is not good for them. There are many people who would have been happier living in developing Africa but they chose to live as third rate citizens in the western world because it just sounds nicer and better to be living on Martin Luther Boulevard, California than to live on a nameless dusty path in Suhum, Eastern Ghana with your address being P. O. Box 6, Suhum.

When you are humble you will not mind being anywhere once your Heavenly Father is there. When you get filled with pride, you will want to live in places because of the name of the place and the perceived wealth and prosperity of that town.

Many people cannot do the work of God because of the things they are conscious of. Through humility you can go to the ends of the world and preach the word of God. Through humility, everywhere will be good enough. But when the pride of life has filled you, you will differentiate between places in your heart. You will be unable to fulfil the great commission.

If you were humble you could sit on the floor, you could live anywhere and you could sleep anywhere. Because you have been led by the pride of life, you will miss the greatness, the crowns and the glory that are meant for humble people.

When you are humble like a child, you worship and dance freely in church. When you lose this humility, you are so conscious of yourself that you cannot worship or dance freely in the house of God. It is a common sight to see the young people surging forward to the front of the church with vigorous dances whilst the mature ones stand aloof and marvel at the energy of the young ones. You may think the young people are dancing because they are youthful. They are actually dancing because they are humble. Pride will keep you fixated by your seat because you are too big for people to see you looking so exuberant and excited.

10. When you are humble like a child, you do not answer back and you do not challenge or argue. When you lose this humility you answer back and challenge.

When a little child is spoken to in his classroom, he does not answer back at his teacher. When his teacher asks him why he is late, he does not say to his teacher, "But you were late yesterday and why are you asking so much about lateness!" It will be completely unheard of for this little child to answer back at his teacher. Indeed, when you are humble like a child you do not challenge your pastors or argue with your fathers.

Watch out for people who challenge, criticise and fight their teachers. These are the sons of pride who have learnt to see faults in grown-ups. These are the ones who have learnt to have an answer for every correction or comment that is made about them.

Marriage is a place where humility can be lost forever. If you were to put a recorder into the bedrooms of many couples you would hear many arguments and retorts, rebukes and rebuttals.

No one is ever wrong and nothing can be said about anything any more. The most obvious errors are challenged and rejected continuously. The bedroom has become the arena for two equally strong and prideful opponents to argue and answer back at each other continuously. Threats of separation and threats of divorce intersperse the never-get-anywhere arguments. Mercy!

Perhaps, a little drop of humility would change the atmosphere at home so much. Perhaps some terminal sickness or some tragic news would change the tone in the bedroom and bring an end to the constant bickering between these sparring partners. A few drops of humility will change the tone and atmosphere of the bedroom.

Do you not think that terminal illness and looming death and the grave would have a humbling effect? Certainly, it will and it does! This is why the bible says we should humble ourselves. We should humble ourselves otherwise we will be humbled. And it is much easier to humble yourself!

11. When you are humble like a child you embrace adventure, excitement and new things. When you lose this humility, you are no longer exciting, adventurous and fearless.

Children love running around and climbing into things to find out what is there. Grown-ups sit back and see everything as risky and dangerous. I remember when we built a bell tower in our church. Before we could fix a trap door, we found children climbing the stairs to the very top. It is quite a scary journey to the top but the children found it great fun to climb all the way to the top. Such is the way and the life of a child.

When you are a child you are ready for the adventure and the excitement that comes with serving God. You are open for a challenge and ready to travel anywhere in search of God's will.

You want to do His will and you want to serve Him no matter where and no matter what it costs. Older Christians, filled with the pride of their middle age and the pride of their achievements do not even read verses that talk about going to the ends of the world.

They do not want to know about the Great Commission. We may call it maturity but it is actually backsliding and pride. The pride of life makes you establish yourself more and more in this life. The pride of life causes you to avoid risky things that may endanger your establishment in this life.

12. When you are humble like a child, you allow yourself to be cared for. When you lose this humility, you want to help yourself.

Children are cared for by their parents, uncles and guardians. They receive care and provision without thinking twice. They somehow feel that the parent or guardian owns the whole world. They do not know where he gets his money from and it does not occur to them to ask. A child allows himself to be provided for. That is humility.

You may ask, "What does this have to do with your spiritual life?" Indeed, when you enter into full time ministry you need to be humble and allow yourself to be looked after by the church. It is a very humbling experience. If you are an educated person who could be gainfully employed anywhere else, it is a humbling experience to allow yourself to be looked after by a congregation.

It is humbling to allow yourself to live off people's benevolence, gifts and offerings. Because I am a medical doctor, I have the option of working in the hospital. It is much more dignified to live off an income that you earned as a specialist surgeon than to live from the collection plate. Without humility you cannot enter into full time ministry. Without humility you cannot work for God. Without humility you will never bear the fruit that God wants you to bear.

13. When you are humble like a child, you are soft and bendable. When you lose this humility, you become hard, unyielding and stubborn.

For rebellion is as the sin of witchcraft, and stubbornness is as iniquity and idolatry. Because thou hast rejected the word of the LORD, he hath also rejected thee from being king.

1 Samuel 15:23

A young tree can be bent easily. An old tree is hard, stubborn and unbendable. The more childlike you are, the more easily you change your mind. The more childlike you are, the more you accept and believe what you are told. Young people flow along easily. The more of an adult you are, the less you change your mind. You must endeavour never to be hard and stubborn because it shows that you have moved away from childlike humility. Hardness and stubbornness are terrible symptoms of pride.

Show me a stubborn woman and I will show you a proud woman! Show me a stubborn and unyielding wife and I will show you a proud wife! Show me a man who will never change, never yield, never accept, never bend and never agree and you are looking at a very proud man. These are not good things! You must do everything to distance yourself from the picture of the unbendable, unyielding, stubborn, hardened, resistant, obstinate and implacable personality!

14. **When you are humble like a child, you are open and transparent. When you lose this humility, you become private, secretive, and closed up.**

> And he said, I heard thy voice in the garden, and I was afraid, because I was naked; and I hid myself.
>
> And he said, Who told thee that thou wast naked? Hast thou eaten of the tree, whereof I commanded thee that thou shouldest not eat?
>
> Genesis 3:10-11

The very first effect of sin was to cover up and become, private, secretive and closed up. Before the evil of pride entered into man he was open and transparent. Sinless man walked about freely in his nakedness, never seeing anything wrong his openness. Hiding, covering secrets and refusing to open up is a sign of great pride. It is when we are adults, and when we have grown out of our childlike humility that we feel too big to show ourselves.

When you are a child you can be naked, and show how and what you really are. But when you are not a child, you reveal less and less of yourself.

Being yourself and revealing who you are, is a sign of childlike humility. You will sense the presence of an evil pride when you sit before a secretive individual who refuses to open up. You can sense that something evil has descended on the person because he or she is unwilling to be open to you any longer.

Do not forget the wonderful blessings of being open. Confessing faults one to another leads to your restoration and healing (James 5:16). Clamping up and keeping your sins covered will not allow you to prosper and receive mercy. "He that covereth his sins shall not prosper: but whoso confesseth and forsaketh them shall have mercy" (Proverbs 28:13). Perhaps the greatest blessing of being open is to have fellowship with others who are equally open. If you walk in the light, as you friend is in the light you have real fellowship with each other. Clamping up, becoming "private and secretive" is the pride that will keep you away from the most important relationships of your life. Pride indeed comes before your fall!

15. When you are humble like a child, you express your need for others. When you lose this humility, you think you do not need anyone.

> God having provided some better thing for us, that they without us should not be made perfect.
>
> Hebrews 11:40

Children are dependent on their parents. Sheep are dependent on their shepherds. Humble pastors are dependent **on other pastors**. I have found out that we do need one another. Everybody needs a little help to get their lives together. As the scripture says, "that they without us are not made perfect" (Hebrews 11:40). This means that no one can be perfect or as great as he should be without others.

If the bible says so, then it is so! You cannot be made perfect unless you depend on someone else.

Most people are glad that they are independent of others. Most people do not want to follow or depend on other people. To be dependent is to be humble.

God wants us to depend on Him and on one another. When you accept that you depend on others, you are being humble. When this humility is deep in your soul, you will embrace the reality of your dependence. Then you will run towards the people that God has determined that you must depend on. It is God who has determined that we should depend on others. Will you accept this? If you do, you are being humble. If you are being humble then you will be lifted up soon.

A child shamelessly calls out for his mother or his father. You will hear him shouting, "Mummy, Mummy, Mummy." You will hear him shouting, "Daddy, Daddy, Daddy." A child shamelessly asks for help when bathing or using the toilet. A child shamelessly asks for help, for food or for money. Every child automatically depends on his parents without thinking. They know they need their parents. They depend on their parents and they accept it.

When you have the humility of a child, you will know in your heart that you depend on God. When you have the humility of a child you will know in your heart that you depend on certain people in this life.

When the spirit of humility is gone, you will start to declare your independence from people around you. You will think to yourself, "I don't need you any more." You may look at your wife and think to yourself, "I don't need her anymore." When the spirit of pride is upon you, you may look at your husband and say to yourself, "I don't need you any more. I am ok without you. After all, what do you really do for me?" These are dangerous thoughts. They are thoughts that are born out of pride. When the spirit of pride is upon a minister, he thinks to himself, "I don't need my spiritual father anymore!" He may say, "I don't need that helper anymore. I can do everything on my own."

You must be very careful about the thoughts you have. Thinking that you don't need anybody to help you is a terrible sign of pride. The prouder you are the more you show that you don't need anyone. A pastor once told me, " I don't need you and you don't need me"! But that is an arrogant statement! The bible says, "that they without us should not be made perfect." We all need each other to be made perfect in ministry.

CHAPTER 3

How To Be Humble Like a Servant

But ye shall not be so: but HE THAT IS GREATEST among you, LET HIM BE AS THE YOUNGER; and he that is chief, AS HE THAT DOTH SERVE.

Luke 22:26

Humility is to make yourself a servant. Jesus linked humility to being a child or being a servant. The art of being a child and the art of being a servant must be studied and meditated upon as long as we live on this earth. Pride is the invisible and dangerous enemy of all of us. The more successful you are the more invisible and the more dangerous pride is. Pride is a specialist at bringing people down. The higher you go, the more attractive you are to the spirit of pride.

It is easy to say to someone, "Be humble" but what exactly should he do to make himself humble? Should he stop smiling? Should he wear old clothes? Should he bow when he is speaking? Should he live in an old house? Should he speak with a soft voice? Should he have a wide sheepish grin every time he speaks? Should he smile when there is nothing to smile at? Should he say "please" before and after each sentence?

I think there are so many opinions about what humility is, but the best person to ask is Jesus. What did Jesus say that we should do in order to be humble? He said we should behave like children or behave like servants.

In the previous chapter I shared about what it means to be humble like a child. In this chapter I want to share with you what it means to be humble like a servant. I need this message as much as everyone who is reading it because I myself am subject, like any other person, to feel good, to feel big and to be pompous.

It is a good thing for us all not to assume that we are humble. It is better to assume that you are proud and fight hard to approach the picture of humility that Jesus taught. Do you look like a servant? Do you talk like a servant? Indeed, many of us who claim to be serving God do not look like servants. We look like lords! We look big, great and pompous! Mercy!

May God help us to leave the picture of worldly pride and begin to look the way Jesus wants us to! Let us now look at the different dimensions of being humble like a servant.

What It Means To Be Humble Like A Servant

1. **When you are humble like a servant, you are happy and willing to do menial jobs. When you lose this humility you are no longer willing to do menial jobs.**

    When they were filled, he said unto his disciples, gather up the fragments that remain, that nothing be lost.

    John 6:12

    ...Elisha the son of Shaphat, which poured water on the hands of Elijah.

    2 Kings 3:11

    When you are humble like a servant you are prepared to do menial jobs. To do a menial job is to be an attendant, a waiter, a cleaner, a security man, a watchman, a factory hand, a secretary, a data officer, a messenger or an odd-job man. These are all menial jobs.

    As you go higher in the Lord you must not think of yourself as being above any job. You must be prepared to work and toil in any capacity, doing mean and lowly jobs. That means you must be prepared to work in the toilet, in the kitchen or on the construction yard. A pastor must be ready to do domestic work and not think that anything is degrading, demeaning or ignoble.

    The scriptures above show us that the apostles were trained by their serving bread and fish to the multitudes. They were also used to gather the crumbs and leftovers after everyone had eaten. Jesus trained His apostles in humility! He trained them in menial jobs and he trained them to be servants.

    Most of us men of God are served and waited on as though we were princes straight out of a palace. Wow! But are we prepared to do the many menial jobs in the house of the Lord? Are we prepared to roll up our sleeves, count the money, take it to the bank, sweep the church, play instruments, clear the compound and do construction work ourselves?

I am amazed when I see pastors who are excellent musicians and singers not using their gifts and skills as musicians any more. They feel that playing instruments and singing with a choir is below their status as ministers of the gospel. What a shame!

There is no work in the house of the Lord that is too low! It is an honour to play an instrument for Jesus! It is an honour to sing in the choir! It is a blessing to have a talent and a gift! Use every gift you have! Do every available job in the house of the Lord! That is what it means to be humble like a servant - do the menial jobs. Never grow out of doing menial jobs.

2. **When you are humble like a servant you are content with meagre or basic conditions for your life. When you lose this humility you no longer accept basic conditions.**

And Jesus said unto him, Foxes have holes, and birds of the air have nests; but the Son of man hath not where to lay his head.

Luke 9:58

Every real servant is content with lowly conditions. Have you heard of a servant who asks for air conditioned rooms and cars before accepting a job? Perhaps you are talking about a different kind of servant! Humble and lowly people who work as servants do not need more than basic conditions to do any job. God wants us to work for Him without making any expensive demands.

This is the reason why large sections of the work of the Lord remain untouched. This is the reason why many parts of the world have no pastor, no evangelist, no prophet or teacher. God's servants require certain conditions before they accept to do the work of the ministry. Unfortunately, most of the souls of the world are found in places where there are only basic conditions!

Since ministers have abandoned the humility of servants, we require much more than average conditions in order to work for the Lord. If you travel through many poor and difficult parts of the world, you will discover how there is an ominous absence of churches.

Indeed, other religions do not mind these basic conditions. Christians, filled with the lust of the eyes, the lust of the flesh and the pride of life, are much more difficult to employ. If ministers become humble like servants again, we will see the greatest harvest ever!

In heaven, our humility will also pay great dividends and we will occupy the greatest thrones reserved for the humble servants of the Lord.

3. **When you are humble like a servant, you are willing to be trained in your work. When you lose this humility you are no longer willing to receive training.**

Better is a poor and a wise child than an old and foolish king, WHO WILL NO MORE BE ADMONISHED.
Ecclesiastes 4:13

The start of a servant's life is his training. You can never be a servant unless you are trained to do things that your master likes and wants. Every master is peculiar and expects specific things from his servants. When you have lost the humility of a servant you cannot be trained or re-trained to do anything. Indeed, it takes humility to be trained.

Without being humble, you cannot be trained – disciplined or instructed to perform certain tasks or tricks for your master. The fact that someone cannot modify your thoughts, behaviour and habits is an indication of your "bigness" and pride. That is what it means to be trained. To be trained means to be pruned, drilled and bent until you are in the desired shape and condition for your master.

When people come to work in a new place, they have to be trained or re-trained. If they feel too big they are often untrainable. They cannot be bended and pruned for their new jobs.

If you want to live a humble life, according to the teachings of Jesus Christ, you must decide to allow yourself to be trained and disciplined to do tasks and tricks for your master. The ability to learn how to behave at work is a sign of humility. The ability to imbibe new things and totally modify your lifestyle is an indication of your humility.

Humility is the key to entering new doors in the kingdom. Many pastors are cut out of new areas of ministry because they are un-trainable in new things. For instance, some people cannot go higher in their music ministry because they will not train to perform new tricks for their master.

Some people cannot enter higher dimensions of the pastoral ministry because they cannot bend down and accept to do the things that are necessary for a change to come. They may read about what to do but pride prevents the old dog from learning new tricks.

Many people read books and are enlightened about new and wonderful things they must experience. But to experience these wonderful things, they would need to be coached, indoctrinated and infused with new ways, new knowledge and new practices. This is where most people get off the train. Pride always cuts short the ministry because humility is a prerequisite for entering the doors of kingdom ministry.

The only thing required of you by your master may be openness and cleanliness. On the other hand, you may work somewhere and the most important thing to your master may be punctuality. Whatever it is, if you cannot bend over and be tutored in that particular area of eccentricity you will never flourish there. Pride is what makes you unable to be a trainable servant.

I have worked with many un-trainable people who eventually did not continue working with me. I have encountered many un-trainable architects, un-trainable contractors, un-trainable lawyers, un-trainable musicians, un-trainable singers, un-trainable engineers, un-trainable television experts and un-trainable computer specialists.

I used to think there was something wrong with me. But as the years have gone by, I found out that I was dealing with the simple problem of pride. I could not discipline and instruct these people in the way that would be pleasing to my ministry.

Most of these people felt they were experts in their field of endeavour and would not listen to the one who was employing them and giving them something to do. Some of them would grumble behind my back and criticise my ideas. They were simply not servants! Their "bigness" and their pride cost them their jobs. Their inflexibility cut short their God-given opportunities and relationships with me.

How sad! May God help us to be servants and to be adaptable and trainable.

4. **When you are humble like a servant, you honour the master God has placed over you. When you lose this humility you do not acknowledge your master any more.**

A son honoureth his father, and a servant his master...
Malachi 1:6

Giving honour is the duty of a servant. People who have lost the humility of Christ find it difficult to honour anyone. If you have the humility of Christ, you will practice the art of honouring those to whom honour is due. So let's ask ourselves, to whom is honour due? Who does the bible say we should honour?

The bible teaches us to honour fathers, mothers, pastors, teachers and masters. If you find it difficult to honour any of these people in your life, you have developed an invisible cloak of pride. Your difficulty in deferring to and honouring these people is the indication that you are not a servant.

If you want to practice humility, forget about developing a wide sheepish grin, smiling at everyone you see and saying "yes please" and "thank you" with every sentence. Begin to honour those to whom honour is due.

I met a pastor who told me how he had not risen very high in ministry because he had failed to honour a man of God.

He said to me, "This man of God was my classmate in Bible School. When we came back to our country, I realised that God's grace was upon him and the Lord began to use him mightily. If I had acknowledged him and honoured him, I would have been part of that wave and move."

He continued, "My ministry would have gone up higher and developed much more than it is today. But I was too big to admit that God was using my classmate more than me."

He unabashedly explained: "My pride has brought me low. I refused to honour him and today he is far ahead in ministry whilst I lag far behind."

"Can't you do that now?" I asked. "Can't you go back, apologise and join him in ministry now?"

But he shook his head and answered sadly, "It's too late. I missed my chance in the ministry. I missed the train."

5. **When you are humble like a servant, you patiently wait for instructions. When you lose this humility, you cannot wait for anything or anyone.**

> For I am a man under authority, having soldiers under me: and I say to this man, Go, and he goeth; and to another, Come, and he cometh; and to my servant, Do this, and he doeth it.
>
> Matthew 8:9

When you have the humility of a servant you will have the patience to wait for instructions. When you have lost the humility of a servant you cannot wait for anything. You cannot wait outside the door. You cannot wait for the meeting to begin. You cannot wait, if there is a delay in the programme. The life of a servant is a life of waiting upon the master's pleasure. When humility has left you, you have no patience, especially for people you think are lesser than you.

Years ago, I wondered about certain individuals who could not wait after meetings to see me. I would be sad and depressed because I really wanted to see them and encourage them to work for the Lord. Sometimes, I would rush out of my office only to realise that they had already left. What I did not realise was that I was dealing with people who did not have the attitude of servants. They were simply not servants. They had no ability to wait.

Even more serious was the reality that the inability to wait revealed a lack of humility. When you come out of a doctor's office, whom do you see in the waiting room? Humble patients waiting to see the doctor! If you are too big to wait, you are too big to be a servant and therefore you are too big to be elevated in the house of God. Today, many people who could not wait have ended up on the spiritual field of barrenness. Watch out for your "inability to wait" for anyone!

Notice your impatience as you blow your horn and scream at other drivers because you can't wait. Notice your irritation with people you think should be faster at what they are doing. Notice your no-nonsense attitude to things you have to wait for. These are indications that you are losing the humble servant's ability to wait.

6. **When you are humble like a servant, you can be sent anywhere. When you lose this humility you are no longer willing to go on certain missions.**

A servant can be sent anywhere. Can you be sent anywhere to do anything for the Lord? Since the church acquired its newfound prosperity, it has become almost impossible to send anyone anywhere. Many of the villages and towns which need missionaries are abandoned because there is no one who can be sent to these places. Indeed, the church is no longer filled with humble servants but with pride-filled house owners and car owners. Our prosperity has made us know the big cities and posh places of the world. Because of this, it is difficult to send anybody anywhere.

The church must be filled again with humble servants who can be sent anywhere to work for God. When this happens, the work of missions will be revived greatly.

7. **When you are humble like a servant, you do not need to be thanked or acknowledged for everything. When you lose this humility you need to be thanked and acknowledged for your contribution.**

> So likewise ye, when ye shall have done all those things which are commanded you, say, We are unprofitable servants: we have done that which was our duty to do.
>
> Luke 17:10

When we have the humility of Christ we will be like the servant who needs no acknowledgment, no praise and no appreciation. The great need to acknowledge people in the house of the Lord is a result of the pride that has seeped into Christianity. When you work for the Lord with the humility of Christ, no one needs to say thank you to you. The fact that your name must be acknowledged at every programme shows how much pride you have. You are far from being a servant when we have to call out your name and mention that you are in church. You are far from being a servant when we have to mention your name in the vote of thanks.

Do you have the need to be acknowledged, honoured and thanked always? If so, then you have forsaken the road of humility.

8. **When you are humble like a servant, you do not need to be seated in a prominent place of honour. When you lose this humility you must be given a prominent place.**

> He must increase, but I must decrease.
>
> John 3:30

When you are a servant you do not need to sit on the high table or the front row. Your strong desire to be seated on the front row reveals your pride.

I once hosted a major programme in which a great man of God came from overseas. During the programme, I invited several pastors from the city to attend. I was amazed at how one of them was offended with me because he had been put on the second row instead of the first row. The hurt in this pastor was so real and so deep. The offence we had caused was to put him on the second row instead of the first. These things are important, and we must honour the men of God. But when we are so concerned about where we sit and where we are positioned, it reveals how much we have departed from servanthood. Never forget that a servant does not need a prominent position in church or at any programme.

9. **When you are humble like a servant, you promote your master in everything. When you lose this humility you are no longer prepared to remain in obscurity.**

For thou hast said in thine heart, I WILL ASCEND into heaven, I will exalt my throne above the stars of God: I will sit also upon the mount of the congregation, in the sides of the north:

Isaiah 14:13

When you are humble like a servant, you will promote your master and not yourself. Servants promote their masters and not themselves.

The master is the one who is known and not the servant. Anyone therefore who promotes himself is not a servant. He has lost the humility that is needed in servanthood.

Do we promote ourselves? Why do want to be known? Is it about us or is it about our Lord? The church is filled with self-promoting ministers. These things reveal a subtle pride that has crept into the ministry.

10. **When you are humble like a servant, you want to serve. When you lose this humility you do not want to serve any more. You want people to serve you.**

And certain women, which had been healed of evil spirits and infirmities, Mary called Magdalene, out of whom went seven devils. And Joanna, the wife of Chuza Herod's steward, and Susanna, and many others, which ministered unto him of their substance.

Luke 8:2-3

What is a servant for? He is there to minister to the needs and wants of others. When you have lost the humility of a servant you do not want to serve anymore but you want to be served. It is important to maintain the attitude of someone who exists to minister and to serve.

So whom shall we serve and whom shall we minister to? We must serve the people God has sent us to. We must do everything we can to give them a better life and to deliver them from the power of darkness. We must bend over backwards and do every menial job that will make the people we are sent to have something better than we did.

Never think of yourself as being better than the people you have been sent to. See the people you are ministering to as great and important. When you see them in the right way you will serve them with the very best of God's blessings.

CHAPTER 4

Mind Not High Things

Be of the same mind one toward another. MIND NOT HIGH THINGS, but condescend to men of low estate. Be not wise in your own conceits.

Romans 12:16

In the ministry of our Lord Jesus Christ you cannot afford to mind high things. People who have minded high things have cut off themselves from true ministry. Perhaps this instruction to mind not high things is one of the most important for ministers of the gospel. Jesus sent us out to preach the gospel to the poor. The gospel of Jesus Christ is received with joy by the poor people of this world.

> Hearken, my beloved brethren, HATH NOT GOD CHOSEN THE POOR of this world rich in faith, and heirs of the kingdom which he hath promised to them that love him?
>
> James 2:5

The poor people of this world do not have all the high things that rich people have. If you are very conscious of high things, it means you are only conscious of the rich. Minding high things will cause you to despise the very people you are called to minister to. Minding high things will cause you to create a class-conscious church. Today, there are churches which are filled with the upper class of the society with no room for the poor whom Christ died for. Every minister of the gospel must be conscious of the lowly things that poor people have to deal with everyday.

It is only a proud heart that thinks about high things and minds high things. This is why the bible teaches us not to mind high things. Minding high things, noticing high things and being conscious of high things is the hallmark of a proud person. Minding high things is not compatible with true ministry! When high things matter so much to you, you cannot be a true minister of the gospel. Why should you be turned away from the people Christ loves?

What Does It Mean to Mind High Things?

1. **Minding high things is to be conscious of the type of car a person drives.**

   Poor people do not have nice cars. If you are very conscious of cars, you will despise someone because of his car. If you are very conscious of cars you will acquire the wrong car at the wrong time.

2. **Minding high things is to be conscious of where a person lives.**

Poor people do not live in nice areas. If you are very conscious of good areas and bad neighbourhoods, you will avoid evangelism in the poor communities. What a poor minister of the gospel you will be because you avoided areas with poor people!

3. **Minding high things is to be conscious of the type of house a person lives in.**

Poor people do not live in nice houses. If you judge people by the type of house they have, you will eliminate most of the people God has sent to you. Poor people do not own nice houses. If you cannot go to lowly houses you are cut out from the important people of your ministry.

4. **Minding high things is to be conscious of whether a person travels first class or economy class.**

Do you travel first class, business class or economy class? Do you judge people's greatness by their class of travel? Then you are minding high things! Stop it now!

5. **Minding high things is to be conscious of people's education in a wrong way.**

"Did you go to this school?" they ask.

"No I did not." Oh, if you did not go to this or that school you are not my type of person. He may not be your type of person but He is God's type. A soul is a soul and is precious to God!

6. **Minding high things is to be conscious of a person's age.**

If you are too conscious of age you are minding high things. God uses young people as well. Actually, young people are very important for the ministry. You will miss the most anointed people if you are only looking for people of a certain age.

> And when the Philistine looked about, and saw David, HE DISDAINED HIM: FOR HE WAS BUT A YOUTH, and ruddy, and of a fair countenance.
>
> 1 Samuel 17:42

7. Minding high things is to be conscious of a person's colour, nationality or tribe.

Our earthly world has divided people into colour groupings. In South Africa, people were once categorised as white, coloured, Indian and black. How unfortunate! Some colours were supposed to be superior to others. How sad! If you become colour conscious, you are minding high things.

If you are conscious of colour, you will have a very limited ministry. There are a few people who are just like you. We agree that your country is great. But if you are so very conscious of your great country, you will put a lot of people off. Also, we may not find so many people from your wonderful tribe in this world. Minding high things is a dangerous thing. It limits the ministry and downsizes the harvest field!

8. Minding high things is to be conscious of the size and profile of somebody's church.

> And Eliab his eldest brother heard when he spake unto the men; and Eliab's anger was kindled against David, and he said, Why camest thou down hither? and with whom hast thou left those FEW SHEEP in the wilderness?
> I know thy pride, and the naughtiness of thine heart; for thou art come down that thou mightest see the battle.
>
> 1 Samuel 17:28

If you assess a ministry by its size, you are minding high things. There may be a small church with a very important message. When you mind high things, you will miss the blessing because you think the church is too small. But there is no church that is too small! Do not despise someone's church because you think there are only poor people there.

"Oh it's not a real church".

"It's just a few Africans."

"Oh it's not a real church".

"It's just a few people from the Philippines".

Dear friend, you are minding high things. You are looking at the wrong parameters! You are conscious of the wrong things!

9. Minding high things is to limit your ministry to places of wealth.

Do you want the blessings of God? Then stop being conscious of high things. Do not let the proud opinions of men guide your ministry away from the places you are needed most.

The high and mighty of this world will ask you;

"Whereabouts is your ministry? Whereabouts is your church? Oh you have a church in Africa?"

"Which city have you been sent to? Atlanta? Orlando? Ooh, that's exciting!"

"Which city have you been sent to? Canchungo? Or Asankragua? Oh dear, where is that? We'll be praying for you."

"Who reads your books, Americans or Africans?"

"Where have you been invited to preach? Berlin? Exciting stuff! Nzerekore? Oh no…! Where is that?"

CHAPTER 5

How To Diagnose "Proud Speaking"

The Lord shall cut off all flattering lips, and THE TONGUE THAT SPEAKETH PROUD THINGS:

Psalms 12:3

What does it mean to have a tongue that speaks proud things? It means you have a mouth that is rude, arrogant and full of pride. There are remarks that are made by proud people which every leader must notice. Pride is revealed when people speak! When you hear certain comments you must ask yourself what have I just heard? Where does this fit in? What kind of statement have I just heard? What is this man saying? Does this statement fit into any of the fifteen categories of proud speaking?

Is what I just heard an over-confident declaration? Is it a comment that has not taken into account the grace of God? Is it a high sounding statement? Is it a rejection of instructions? Is it the illegitimate rebuking of an authority? Is it correction upwards? Is it a proud person abruptly ending a conversation? Is it a proud declaration of self-sufficiency? Is it a statement that trivialises an important issue? Is it a statement that belittles others? Is this mockery and despising laughter? Is it a statement of inflexibility and rigidity? Is it a declaration of personal greatness? Is it unwillingness to apologise? Is it a threat?

In this section, we are going to study the different types of "proud speaking" so you can identify them for yourself. Your antennae must go up when you notice certain comments.

Fifteen Types of "Proud Speaking"

1. OVERCONFIDENT DECLARATIONS:

And went again into the judgment hall, and saith unto Jesus, Whence art thou? But Jesus gave him no answer.

Then saith Pilate unto him, Speakest thou not unto me? KNOWEST THOU NOT THAT I HAVE POWER TO CRUCIFY THEE, and have power to release thee?

Jesus answered, THOU COULDEST HAVE NO POWER AT ALL AGAINST ME, except it were given thee from above: therefore he that delivered me unto thee hath the greater sin.

John 19:9-11

Watch out for people who make these over confident declarations about who they are and what they can do. Pontius Pilate mistakenly told Jesus that he had power to arrest him and power to release him. But Jesus rightly pointed out to him that he would have no power unless God had given it to him. In other words he actually had no power!

All the abilities that you have are actually God-given talents and abilities. You must be careful to acknowledge this reality. Any declaration that leaves out or forgets the divine factor is an over confident declaration of pride.

Some years ago, I had a pastor leaving the pastoral staff. Among the many things he said was one outstanding statement. He said, "*I will show you church growth in six months.*" In other words, "*I will show you how I can make a church grow very quickly, in six months.*" Indeed, it has been many years since that statement was made. That was indeed an over confident declaration. But dear friend, remember the scripture where Paul said, "I planted, Apollos watered but God gave the increase." God is the only one who can show us church growth in six months!

2. COMMENTS THAT FORGET THE GRACE OF GOD

Watch out for people who speak as though they accomplish all that they do without God's grace. Do not describe God's gifts to you as though they were your own achievements.

One day at a meeting, pastors were being urged to go out on visitation. A lady stood up and encouraged everyone to fulfil the great commission. Suddenly, a brother blurted out from the back, "*You don't have a husband or a child that is why you are urging us to go out on evangelism.*"

That was an unfortunate comment by someone who had a spouse and a child. "For who maketh thee to differ *from another*? And what hast thou that thou didst not receive? Now if thou didst receive it, why dost thou glory, as if thou hadst not received it?" (1 Corinthians 4:7) Do not forget that it takes the grace of God to get married. It also takes the grace of God to have a child.

3. HIGH-SOUNDING STATEMENTS

> And thou his son, O Belshazzar, hast not humbled thine heart, though thou knewest all this;
>
> But hast lifted up thyself against the Lord of heaven; and they have brought the vessels of his house before thee, and thou, and thy lords, thy wives, and thy concubines, have drunk wine in them; and THOU HAST PRAISED THE GODS OF SILVER, AND GOLD, OF BRASS, IRON, WOOD, and stone, which see not, nor hear, nor know: and the God in whose hand thy breath is, and whose are all thy ways, hast thou not glorified:
>
> Daniel 5:22-23

There are people who make high-sounding statements. These high-sounding statements reveal a well of pride. When Belshazzar praised the gods of gold and silver, he revealed an arrogance that deserved the coming punishment. He declared that his sustenance came from the gold and the silver and the wood and the stone. He did not want or need the living God!

A young man said to me once, *"Do you know how much I earn? I can never pay tithes."* He was so full of his achievements and his successes that he boasted that he would never pay tithes. He found out later, though, that it was God who had given him the strength to earn so much money. When he became terminally ill, he came to my office and declared his readiness to pay tithes. His earlier high-sounding statement about tithes was no longer valid.

One day, we approached a newly appointed government official. I needed to see him about something important. When he got the message that we needed to see him, he blurted out, *"My O my! This post that I have been given! These pastors are worrying me everyday because I have been given this position."*

Instead of feeling honoured that pastors wanted to see him, he was rather exasperated at the thought of having to entertain us. We quickly aborted our visit and he missed the blessing that he would have had from the servants of the Lord.

4. STATEMENTS THAT REJECT AND REFUSE INSTRUCTIONS

> And Moses sent to call Dathan and Abiram, the sons of Eliab; and they said, WE WILL NOT COME UP
>
> Numbers 16:12

Watch out for people who abruptly reject and refuse instructions. Moses encountered proud people who told him flatly, "We will not come." These people did not end up well because pride comes before a fall. They were soon swallowed up by the ground. Such is the fate of those who lift themselves up haughtily.

I once sent a pastor out as a missionary. When he came back from his mission, I called for an extraordinary meeting and asked him to come to the office. This pastor was so irritated by my request that he sent me a message through the person I had sent to call him. His message was simple, *"I will not come for your meeting. You can do what you want. I will not come."*

Does that sound familiar? Indeed, it sounds just like Korah and his friends in the book of Numbers.

As our church developed, we organised special assessment and accountability conferences for all pastors and leaders in sections of the church. The meetings were characterized by healthy debates, questioning and probing of the different pastors as to whether they were doing their work well or not.

However, it did not go down well with everyone. One pastor said, "I will not attend the assessment and accountability conference. I am not a small boy! Why should I go to such a meeting for small boys to ask me questions!"

As pastors become proud, they become more independent. I remember one pastor who said, *"We now have our own diocese, we will not go to the headquarters for meetings."*

Does that sound familiar? Again it does! It sounds just like Korah who said he would not go up for the meeting. Watch out, your end will be like Korah!

5. ILLEGITIMATE REBUKES OF AUTHORITIES

And they gathered themselves together against Moses and against Aaron, and said unto them, Ye take too much upon you, seeing all the congregation are holy, every one of them, and the LORD is among them: WHEREFORE THEN LIFT YE UP YOURSELVES ABOVE THE CONGREGATION OF THE LORD?

And when Moses heard it, he fell upon his face:

Numbers 16:3-4

Watch out for people who rebuke spiritual authorities. It is a dangerous practice and a sign of loftiness, haughtiness, arrogance and pride. The sons of Korah rose up and rebuked Moses. They accused him of being puffed up. Imagine that! Imagine telling Moses that he feels too big! Then they rebuked him for having too much power in the camp of Israel. They also pointed out to him that he was not the only holy or special person in Israel. In their presentation, they made it clear that other people in the congregation were holy. To be holy means to be special. Imagine that!

There are always people who are ready and willing to rebuke spiritual authorities. There are politicians who lift up themselves and speak disparagingly about God's servants. There are pastors who rise up and point out faults of the experienced spiritual fathers of the day. Watch out for people who can fearlessly rebuke those who have laid the foundations of the church.

On one occasion, I visited a friend who was a minister of the gospel. I went along with a spiritual father who was also a father to the minister I was visiting. This minister of the gospel was living in error and was struggling under the weight of many wrong decisions he had taken. It was only because the Lord had directed me that I had decided to offer my help.

The spiritual father I had gone along with also began to counsel this brother who was steeped in error. I thought that the presence of this spiritual father would make all the difference to this meeting, but I was wrong. To my utter amazement, the gentleman began to shout, *"Who do you think you are? What do you mean by coming to my house to talk to me like this? What do you mean by coming to my house without prior notice? Why didn't you give me notice that you were coming here?"*

We sat in utter amazement as he spilled out his vituperations. The final shock came when he stood up and walked out the spiritual father and myself. *"Go out of my house"*, he exclaimed. He rebuked us as we walked through the door and said, *"Next time you are coming to my house, come with more sense"*.

I felt so embarrassed that I had subjected this spiritual father to such humiliation. I do not think it is a spirit of humility that tells a spiritual father "to speak with more sense."

6. CORRECTION UPWARDS: POINTING OUT THE ERRORS OF ELDERS

> From that time forth began Jesus to shew unto his disciples, how that he must go unto Jerusalem, and suffer many things of the elders and chief priests and scribes, and be killed, and be raised again the third day.
>
> THEN PETER TOOK HIM, AND BEGAN TO REBUKE HIM, saying, Be it far from thee, Lord: this shall not be unto thee.
>
> But he turned, and said unto Peter, Get thee behind me, Satan: thou art an offence unto me: for thou savourest not the things that be of God, but those that be of men.
>
> Matthew 16:21-23

Peter tried to correct Jesus Christ. Peter tried to guide Jesus Christ in His ministry. Watch out for people who correct pastors and tell them what to do. This is what Peter tried to do when he told Jesus not to die on the cross.

Can you imagine what would have happened to us if Jesus had listened to Peter's uninformed counsel? We would all have been sitting in darkness waiting to go to hell. A sheep is not supposed to direct the shepherd. It is the shepherd who directs the sheep. Peter became over confident because of his appointment as the head of the church. He began to rebuke the king of kings and the Lord of Lords and to tell Him what to do.

Watch out for people who are so big that they know what the pastor must teach and how he must teach it. I have had church members who have corrected my preaching after I delivered the sermon.

Someone once told me to hurry up with my message. "*You repeat yourself too much*" she said to me. Another person also said my sermons were too long. Others said they were too short. Some of my congregants said there were too many stories. I once had some medical students who rebuked me for teaching too long on the subject of tithing. I became so discouraged by their rebukes that it took a vision from God to make me write on the subject of tithing.

On another occasion I had a powerful lady church member rebuking me for the way I was running the worldwide church. "*That's not the way to run the church! That's not the way to do it.*" I had to point out to her that I was running the church on a full time basis whilst she was only coming to church twice a week. Surely, I would know a little more about running the church than she did? Delusions and deceptions are the foundations of all forms of arrogance and haughtiness.

Some newly born again Christians had a meeting to question my calling. They were not sure whether God had really called me to preach or not. I marvelled, because, a few days earlier I had led some of them to Christ and laid hands on them to receive the Holy Spirit. Why on earth were they questioning my calling when God had used me to help them to receive the Holy Spirit? Sometimes, the emptiest barrels make the most noise.

On another occasion, a pastor told me over the phone, "*Why don't you make up your mind on what you want us to do? When you tell us to do one thing and we start doing it, then you come up with something else"*. He rebuked me for giving new instructions all the time. *"Make up your mind!"* he shouted over the phone.

Watch out for people who are behaving just like Peter did. Because of their recent appointments and minimal spiritual gains, they think they are something that they are not. What happened to Peter when he rebuked his master? He fell so low! God revealed to him that he was actually nothing!

7. ABRUPTLY ENDING CONVERSATIONS

> We have heard of the pride of Moab; he is very proud: even of his haughtiness, and his pride...
>
> Isaiah 16:6

Abruptly ending phone conversations and cutting the phone are indications of haughtiness and pride. Slamming a phone on someone is even worse. To be haughty means to show arrogant superiority to someone. It also means to disdain someone you see as unworthy. It is only when you view someone as unworthy of your time that you would end the conversation abruptly and slam the phone.

I once made a call to a pastor who was being tempted by the enemy to fall into error. When I asked a couple of questions and pointed out to the pastor that he was in error, he refused to continue speaking. Any questions I asked him from that point onwards were not answered. *There was silence at the other end of the phone as this pastor, whom I had ordained into the ministry, brought the conversation to an abrupt end.* I could not believe my ears when the conversation ended. Indeed, I sensed the haughtiness and the disdain for my opinion.

I once spoke to someone who claimed to be my daughter. I pointed out to her that if she were really my daughter she would obey what I was saying. It is easy to say you are a son or a daughter. Saying you are a son or a daughter is not the same as being humble.

When you actually obey someone you claim is your father, you prove that you are occupying the seat of a son or a daughter. Indeed, this lady was not acting like a daughter but like a "big Madam" who knew everything. She had her own opinions about everything. She had answers and rebuttals to all my requests. Was that a daughter? That was a woman, my equal! She stood up to me eyeball-to-eyeball, point-to-point and challenged me all the way! She gave me a good run for my money and she never obeyed me. Does your child behave like that? Certainly not! A child will say, "Yes Mummy" and "Yes Daddy" and do what you say!

8. DECLARATIONS OF SELF-SUFFICIENCY

> How much she hath glorified herself, and lived deliciously, so much torment and sorrow give her: FOR SHE SAITH IN HER HEART, I SIT A QUEEN, AND AM NO WIDOW, AND SHALL SEE NO SORROW.
>
> Therefore shall her plagues come in one day, death, and mourning, and famine; and she shall be utterly burned with fire: for strong is the Lord God who judgeth her.
>
> Revelation 18:7-8

Watch out for great and swelling words of self-sufficiency. The queen of Revelation 18 was full of herself. She thought her situation would never change. You must notice when people speak great swelling words of self-sufficiency.

I once visited a pastor who had offended me and whom I had offended. I spoke to him with kind words and suggested that we forget our differences and become friends again. I was taken aback by his response. In the heat of his anger he said many things. But one thing he said stood out:

"I don't need you for anything. I don't need you and you do not need me."

But that was not true. I did need him and he did need me. By declaring that he did not need me, he was speaking great swelling words of self-sufficiency and independence. The bible teaches us that we need one another. Be careful of speaking prideful words!

9. STATEMENTS THAT TRIVIALISE ISSUES

And Eliab his eldest brother heard when he spake unto the men; and Eliab's anger was kindled against David, and he said, Why camest thou down hither? And WITH WHOM HAST THOU LEFT THOSE FEW SHEEP in the wilderness? I know thy pride, and the naughtiness of thine heart; for thou art come down that thou mightest see the battle.

1 Samuel 17:28

The brothers of king David mocked at David's job of feeding the sheep. They also mocked at the number of sheep that David had. It was insignificant as far as they were concerned. David was not an important person because he was looking after a few sheep. These are dangerous attitudes and they are dangerous because they are the attitudes of pride.

Often, the things you trivialise or marginalise can turn out to be very important. Years ago, when we began our church, I had people mocking me for having little churches. They made fun of our branches and said, *"There is nothing to them. It is just two or three people."* Just as David was mocked for having a few sheep, I was also mocked for having a few sheep. It is amazing that these few sheep have grown into thousands. Watch out for the things that you trivialise, minimise and marginalise.

Watch out for pastors who are too big to talk to young people! Watch out for pastors who are too big to find out why the church toilet does not work! Watch out for pastors who are too big to find out why their church's website is not functioning! Watch out for pastors who are too big to go to their church's building site. Watch out for pastors who are only interested in how much money came in but not how it is counted! Watch out for people who do not know how or who cleans the church! There are often pastors who belittle important jobs and important people. You must be careful because what you minimise, trivialise and marginalise may be the most important thing in your ministry.

Trivialising Hurts

Don't trivialise someone's hurts and offences. I once visited a man of God I respected. I visited him because I wanted to develop a relationship with him. When I sat in this man of God's office, I told him why I had come. First of all, I wanted to clear up an issue in which this pastor had said negative things about us. It had been a very painful experience to hear him denigrate us and despise us because of the good relationship we had had with him for years.

On bringing up the issue, he reacted with extreme exasperation, *"What are you talking about? "He asked. "I don't remember what you are saying. I don't even remember such an event. How do you expect me to remember something that happened so long ago."*

We felt so stupid for even bringing up the issue. We also felt silly for even trying to relate to someone so great! My associate and I left that office with our tails between our legs, never to return.

We were the most insignificant and unimportant visitors to that man of God's office. We grinned like embarrassed sheep as we left the company of that great man of God. Indeed, our relationship was broken forever. We felt obtuse and brainless for having even tried to relate with these powerful men.

Perhaps, an important spiritual relationship and link was broken. Who knows what good would have come out of our relationship if only we had not been made to feel so dim-witted by this exasperated man of God. Many years later, this pastor fell into great difficulty and lost his church and position. I was surprised to see him standing in the congregation and looking at me in awe as I laid the foundation for one of our cathedrals.

10. STATEMENTS THAT BELITTLE OTHERS

> And Rabshakeh said unto them, Say ye now to Hezekiah, Thus saith the great king, the king of Assyria, What confidence is this wherein thou trustest?
>
> I say, sayest thou, (but they are but vain words) I have counsel and strength for war: now on whom dost thou trust, that thou rebellest against me?
>
> Lo, thou trustest in the staff of this broken reed, on Egypt; whereon if a man lean, it will go into his hand, and pierce it: so is Pharaoh king of Egypt to all that trust in him.
>
> Isaiah 36:4-6

Watch out for people who feel so big and arrogant that they belittle everyone around them. Rabshekah came up to the Israelites and threatened them with war. He despised and belittled the Israelites. He mocked at the help they were going to receive from Egypt. He told them that they were leaning on a staff that was a broken reed. Watch out for people who consider things to be below them.

I remember a pastor who was above the many little jobs that were done in the church. If you wanted to contact him you would have to speak with his wife. He just could not find the time to speak to you. Perhaps you may think this pastor had four thousand members and therefore was too busy to make certain appointments himself. He actually had only about forty members. Here again, you wonder where the pomposity and arrogance came from. He would say, *"If you want to tell me anything, speak to my wife or my secretary."*

He would turn away and walk off, unable to speak to the little ones. Perhaps you may think the little ones I am referring to were the congregants of his church. No, they were not. They were other pastors who belonged to the same ministry. Watch out for pastors who consider everyone else too little, too small or too insignificant to be spoken to.

11. STATEMENTS THAT MOCK AND LAUGH AT OTHER PEOPLE

Tell it not in Gath, publish it not in the streets of Askelon; lest the daughters of the Philistines rejoice, lest the daughters of the uncircumcised triumph.

2 Samuel 1:20

The scripture teaches us not to spread the stories of bad news of our brothers. Tell it not in Gath and publish it not in the streets of Askelon! Why must we not publish it? Because God does not want the Philistines to rejoice against the people of the Lord! God does not want the daughters of the uncircumcised to triumph over us. It is wrong to laugh at fallen brothers. It is wrong to continually expose them and to ridicule them.

I once had a vision in which the Lord showed me the pride of pastors. This was a vision of something that had happened in front of me. The Lord said to me, "Watch this. This is pride and it has devastating effects."

There was a pastor who fell into sin. He had many spiritual problems and also had numerous affairs with women in the church. Because of the scandal, several members of his church migrated and joined other churches. This broken pastor was left with very few members.

Many churches benefitted from the influx of this pastor's members. However, there was a church that was pastored by a group of confident and anointed ministers. One day, the confident pastors asked their congregation, *"How many of you came from that broken pastor's church?"* Several people lifted up their hands.

One of the senior pastors made these migrant members stand up. He then recounted the problems in the church of the broken pastor and told the members publicly that they needed to be cleansed from the sins and evils of the church they were coming from. He pointed out that they had been polluted and affected because of the sins of that broken pastor. He promised to organise cleansing and sanctification for them.

In a flash, the Lord showed me the church of this righteous pastor divided and scattered. He said to me, "That is pride; to stand up, to rebuke and to ridicule a broken pastor and his church members publicly is to forget that you are just a man. Indeed, I stood amazed as the vision played out over the years. The people who mocked at the broken pastor fell into the same sins and difficulties themselves.

Watch out for people who mock and laugh at others when they are down and in difficulty. It is arrogance and over confidence to make fun of people who have fallen into difficulty!

Some years ago, I visited a wonderful ministry in a far away land. This was a wonderful church with a large and growing congregation. The pastors of this church were young, successful, dynamic men. I visited the bookshop of this church and was impressed by the books. I think I actually bought a book from that bookshop. By God's grace I was able to meet the senior pastor of the church.

I interacted with him and we exchanged some niceties in the corridor of the church. As we were about to depart we prayed and everyone asked that I say a prayer. I prayed powerfully from the depths of my heart. When I said "Amen", I was immediately confronted by the pastors of that church. They asked me what I meant by praying for humility.

Honestly, I had not been conscious of the fact that I was praying for humility. Actually I had been studying about the virtues of humility and it was just bubbling in my heart.

I actually did not think these pastors were proud. It did not even occur to me that they needed humility. I thought they were great pastors and I prayed for what I thought was the best and highest extra quality that a pastor could ever have – humility.

"What do you mean?" they asked. "Who told you that we are proud? Do you think we need humility? Are you trying to tell

us something? What do you mean by that? You just walk into a church and start praying that people should be humble! He thinks he is spiritual. Very funny! Praying for us to be humble!"

I was shocked and amazed as they rebuked and ridiculed me for praying for them to have humility. I was virtually walked out of that church and I knew that my friendship with those wonderful pastors would not develop. But perhaps they should have received my prayers better than they did. There were storms on the way, and the next time I heard of them they were in prison for various crimes.

Watch out for people who mock and laugh. Mocking and laughing at people is not a good sign. It speaks of arrogance and haughtiness.

12. DECLARATIONS OF PERSONAL GREATNESS AND ACHIEVEMENTS

All this came upon the king Nebuchadnezzar.
At the end of twelve months he walked in the palace of the kingdom of Babylon.
The king spake, and said, IS NOT THIS GREAT BABYLON, THAT I HAVE BUILT for the house of the kingdom by the might of my power, and for the honour of my majesty?
While the word was in the king's mouth, there fell a voice from heaven, saying, O king Nebuchadnezzar, to thee it is spoken; The kingdom is departed from thee.
Daniel 4:28-31

Watch out for people who speak about their achievements as though their own hand and power has accomplished them.

Nebuchadnezzar made the mistake of speaking of his achievements in the wrong way. He was full of himself and his achievements.

I once asked a woman if she believed in God. She said, *"I believe in myself. I work hard and I do not harm anyone. I believe in myself."* I believe I was actually hearing the voice of the devil who has possessed millions of Europeans and caused them to cast out the memory and the knowledge of God. Watch out for the pride of the western world that has forsaken the reality of God. You will soon see the effect of this pride.

"I" and "We"

Once I was buying some equipment for our church. As I negotiated with the Jewish owner of the business, he rebuked me and said I was speaking in the wrong way.

"Why do you rebuke me?" I asked.

He said, *"You keep on saying 'I am going to do this. I am going to use this equipment for that. I will come here tomorrow. I will do this and that'"*.

He said to me, *"Don't say 'I' say 'we'!"*

He explained, *"'I' is for God and 'we' is for human beings."*

He continued, *"I am that I am is Jehovah. It is only God who can say, 'I will do this', 'I will go here and there'."* I took note of that rebuke and I realised how true it was.

Indeed, it was Lucifer who said, *"I will arise, I will ascend the throne, I will replace God, I will fight God."* You will notice how Lucifer used the word "I" on five different occasions. Lucifer, full of himself and full of pride, was deluded into thinking that he could fight God who had created him.

> For thou hast said in thine heart, I will ascend into heaven, I will exalt my throne above the stars of God: I will sit also upon the mount of the congregation, in the sides of the north:
> I will ascend above the heights of the clouds; I will be like the most High.
>
> Isaiah 14:13-14

I have met lay pastors who have said in their hearts, *"What is the use of full time ministry?"* After all, I have a bigger church than the full time pastor. Again these are all thoughts of arrogance. People, who do not understand what they are doing and why they achieve what they achieve, speak with great swelling words of pride. Watch out for people who do not understand that it is God's grace that makes the difference.

13. DECLARATIONS SHOWING UNWILLINGNESS TO APOLOGISE

> Saying, I have sinned in that I have betrayed the innocent blood. And they said, what is that to us? See thou to that. And he cast down the pieces of silver in the temple, and departed, and went and hanged himself.
>
> Matthew 27:4-5

One of the greatest manifestations of pride is the unwillingness to say "sorry" or to apologise. Judas Iscariot was unwilling to say sorry. He never apologised to Jesus for what he did. He also never apologised to the other disciples. In fact he did not even want to see them again.

Watch out for people who cannot say sorry! Watch out for people who cannot turn around! Watch out for people who cannot do a one hundred and eighty degrees turn when they are going in the wrong direction.

I once encountered a pastor who said, *"I will not apologise to my overseer."* Even though he was wrong, he would not say sorry. Pride would not allow him to lower himself and acknowledge that he was wrong.

Over the years, I have realised that the inability to say sorry or to apologise is one of the cardinal signs of pride. My experience shows me that the hardest and most rebellious people never say sorry!

14. DECLARATIONS OF RIGIDITY AND UNMOVEABILITY

> And Moses went out from Pharaoh, and intreated the LORD. And the LORD did according to the word of Moses; and he removed the swarms of flies from Pharaoh, from his servants, and from his people; there remained not

one. And Pharaoh hardened his heart at this time also, NEITHER WOULD HE LET THE PEOPLE GO.

Exodus 8:30-32

Pharaoh was hard and unyielding. His pride led to his downfall. When people declare, "*I will never change. I will never agree!*" They are making declarations of rigidity and immovability. These are dangerous words and filled with pride. They are the biggest symptoms and signs of pride you can have in a person.

I once met a lady who told me that she was unwilling to follow her husband. She said to me, "*I am fiercely independent!*" Wow, what a statement! It was no wonder that she was soon divorced. To be fiercely independent is to declare yourself incompatible with marriage. It is also the same as declaring yourself ready to fall into divorce.

I once met a man who escaped from hell by the skin of his teeth. On my first encounter with him he said to me, "*I will never be born again and I will never change.*" He rebuked me for my sermon on being born again and made it clear that he would never respond to such a message.

However, ten years later I encountered this same gentleman at a programme. I preached on the same subject, You Must Be Born Again. However this time, he raised his hand and gave his life to Christ. I could not believe that the same gentleman who had displayed such rigidity was now yielding to the spirit of God.

Be careful of rigidity! Be careful of the unmoveable posture. Be careful of the posture of hardness. It is the posture of pride!

15. THREATENING STATEMENTS

And spake to them after the counsel of the young men, saying, My father made your yoke heavy, and I will add to your yoke: my father also chastised you with whips, but I will chastise you with scorpions.

1 Kings 12:14

Watch out for people who threaten you. It is usually a sign of over confidence. When Rehoboam threatened to whip his citizens with scorpions, he was treading on dangerous ground. He was confident in power that he actually did not have.

Unfortunately, pride is often based on some kind of delusion or deception. We sometimes feel over confident in our righteousness. What we do not realise is that the things we are able to do are because of the grace of God. When you start threatening people, it is because you think you have some kind of power that you do not have.

I have been threatened by many people in my ministry. I was once threatened by a witch whilst I was preaching. She kept throwing things at me and opposing what I was saying. She was exerting powers that she did not have.

On another occasion, I was threatened by a group of young men who wanted our church to leave their community. Insults were hurled at me. Insults were hurled at the one who gave birth to me. Curses have been rained on me by individuals who felt I was not worthy of being a pastor.

On yet another occasion, I was threatened by a pastor who did not want me to have a church in a particular city. He sent me a message and his message was clear, "*I will drive you out of this town.*" He threatened to write a book about me that would be so damaging that I would not be able to continue my missionary work in that city. Wow!

These are threatening words of arrogance from men who are puffed up with delusions of grandeur. Be careful in your personal life when you threaten people around you! I will drive you out. I will finish you. I will clear you from there! Careful now! It is always a sign of pride!

CHAPTER 6

What it Means To Have A Proud Look

A PROUD LOOK, a lying tongue, and hands that shed innocent blood

Proverbs 6:17

A proud look is a facial expression, posture or presence that communicates arrogance and superiority. Is there something you can see on the outside of someone who is proud? Amazingly, it is possible to see pride when you look at a person. Sometimes it is possible to feel pride when you are in the presence of a proud person. The bible calls this a "proud look" or a "high look".

"Whoso privily slandereth his neighbour, him will I cut off: him that hath AN HIGH LOOK and a proud heart will not I suffer" (Psalms 101:5).

"A proud look" is what you *see* and experience when you are in the presence of someone who is proud. The words "proud" and "look" come from the Hebrew words "*rum*" and "*aiyn*". "*Rum*" means lofty, high, uplifted exalted and raised. "*Aiyn*" means face, presence. What does that give us? A proud look is a high uplifted, exalted, raised, lofty, face or presence.

Four Ways To Identify A Proud Look

1. A proud look is FACIAL EXPRESSION that reveals pride.

A proud look is the expressionless face of a person who is not interested or impressed with what is going on.

A high look is also a look of aloofness. These proud and aloof people are not concerned, not interested and not impressed with you.

A proud look is revealed when a person does not smile, clap, say amen or show approval during a service.

A proud look is revealed when a person looks away while you are talking to him.

A proud look is revealed when a person does not bend his neck or turn his head in your direction when he is speaking to you.

I remember a pastor who had a classic "high look". This pastor with the "high look" said very little at meetings. He would hardly communicate or say much. That did not mean that his pride could not be diagnosed. In fact, the high look made me feel uneasy in his presence.

It is this aloofness and indifference that we call a proud look. One day, this brother got into difficulty and instead of apologising and going through the correction meted out to him, he just walked away without a word. He was too big to apologise and he was too big to be transferred to a new location.

Indeed, without a word of apology or a word of thank you, he vanished from our lives. He did not bother to say a word to those who loved him! Pride got the better of him as he walked away to the amazement of his spiritual fathers and mentors.

2. A proud look is AN ATTITUDE that exudes arrogance.

The wicked, through THE PRIDE OF HIS COUNTENANCE, will not seek after God: God is not in all his thoughts.

Psalms 10:4

A person with a proud look has an attitude that you feel in all your communication to him. It is an attitude you would feel in every kind of interaction with this fellow.

For instance, you may send him a text but he would not respond even though he had seen it. You would send him an email but he would not reply even though he knew you were waiting for a reply. You would call him but he would not respond to your calls. Even if he did respond to your calls it would be so much later. You would get a sense that your communication to him was not important to him. A humble person would call back immediately and apologise for missing the call.

Watch out for people with a proud attitude. You can feel it through their texts and calls.

3. **A proud look is A POSTURE that communicates pride and generates contention.**

   Only by pride cometh contention: ...

   Proverbs 13:10

The presence of this invisible evil is best revealed by the presence of contention. Quarrelling and contention are the best signs of the presence of pride. Quarrelling, bitterness and unforgiveness are always signs of pride. A lofty presence always brings conflict! "He that is of a proud heart stirreth up strife..." (Proverbs 28:25).

Why is contention a sign of pride? Because contention or fighting only occurs between two parties who see themselves as equally matched or almost equally matched.

When a person sees himself as a junior or a subordinate, he would rarely engage in any kind of conflict. Therefore, congregants rarely quarrel with their pastors. Pupils rarely quarrel with their teachers. Secretaries rarely quarrel with their bosses. Employees rarely have any form of open contention with their employers.

However, when the junior party begins to feel "big", contention and quarrels begin. Only by pride cometh contention! Girl friends hoping to be married to the man of God rarely contend or quarrel with him. Newly betrothed wives rarely contend with their spouses. However as time passes and familiarity sets in, submissive and humble brides become hard, unyielding and accusative. Pride is manifest through the accusations, the unyielding hardness and the contention.

Associate pastors rarely contend with their senior pastor when they see him as a great man of God and truly anointed by the spirit.

However, when they feel that they are also called of God and they also know a thing or two about the ministry, there is always contention and strife. When the senior pastor stands in the presence of a pride-filled associate, he senses the pride. Because there is a proud look! It is not easy to tell when there is a proud look. But the coming of contention settles the question. Pride always generates contention and strife! Once there is strife there is pride!

4. A proud look is A PRESENCE that communicates superiority.

Another area where a proud look is a detected is where a person has racist pride. When a person starts to speak about a country in which he lives or in which he is forced to live in a certain way, you can sense the heart of despisement.

When a person is postured against a certain country and sees nothing good, you can sense the beginnings of racial superiority. After a while, such a person exudes despisement of all that he sees and experiences in that country. Such people are not good missionaries because they despise the people to whom they have been sent.

For instance someone from another continent may say in a despising tone, *"You better watch your bags, there are many Africans here."* Someone else may say, *"Mr Jack and Jill are very African"*. Another person may say, *"These African men are boring"*. *"Be careful you do not touch any of these dirty African places"*. These statements reveal a feeling of despisement from someone who feels superior.

I have worked with many people from many countries and I have noticed this proud look in people who did not have the missionary spirit. Watch out for a proud look in every foreigner you meet! Watch out for the proud look in yourself every time you are among people of a different race.

CHAPTER 7

Humble Yourself Means "Do it yourself"

Humble YOURSELVES in the sight of the Lord, and he shall lift you up.

James 4:10

Likewise, ye younger, submit yourselves unto the elder. Yea, all of you be subject one to another, and be CLOTHED WITH HUMILITY: for God resisteth the proud, and giveth grace to the humble.

1 Peter 5:5

"**Do** it yourself" is an important concept that saves money and time for human beings today. In many countries it is expensive to hire a carpenter or a plumber. You are better off if you go to a "DIY" shop and learn to repair your bed yourself.

The Agents Of Humility

The same thing applies to humility. God asks you to do it yourself! He asks you to humble yourself. In other words, do the humbling and lowering things yourself. The alternative to humbling yourself is not a nice one. If you do not humble yourself there are other agents who will do it for you.

The Bible describes various unpleasant agents of humility. These unpleasant agents of humility are standing by to induce humility in our lives. Paul the apostle had his fair share of these unpleasant agents.

> And LEST I SHOULD BE EXALTED above measure through the abundance of the revelations, there was given to me A THORN IN THE FLESH, the messenger of Satan to buffet me, lest I should be exalted above measure.
>
> For this thing I besought the Lord thrice, that it might depart from me.
>
> And he said unto me, My grace is sufficient for thee: for my strength is made perfect in WEAKNESS. Most gladly therefore will I rather glory in my INFIRMITIES, that the power of Christ may rest upon me.
>
> "Therefore I take pleasure in infirmities, in REPROACHES, in NECESSITIES, in PERSE-CUTIONS, in DISTRESSES for Christ's sake: for when I am weak, then am I strong.
>
> 2 Corinthians 12:7-10

When God blesses a person with an abundance of grace and gifts, whether physical or spiritual, there is a great tendency to be lifted up with pride. Lucifer was lifted up with pride in this way and it destroyed him. Unfortunately, most of us are not able to humble ourselves and prevent self-destruction without agents of humility.

For this reason, the Lord is often forced to allow unpleasant agents of humility to come into our lives. Paul called this agent a "thorn in the flesh".

Indeed, sometimes, God blesses people so much that it is impossible for them to remain humble. You will notice that most people who have a lot of money and earthly blessings are no longer humble enough to be good Christians. The wise man who wrote the book of Proverbs knew this reality. He even prayed that he would not have too much money because he knew that riches could destroy him through pride.

> Remove far from me vanity and lies: GIVE ME NEITHER POVERTY NOR RICHES; feed me with food convenient for me:
> LEST I BE FULL, AND DENY THEE, and say, Who is the Lord? or lest I be poor, and steal, and take the name of my God in vain.
>
> Proverbs 30:8-9

Reproaches, necessities, needs and difficulties come to help you remember that you are a man. Your riches, your achievements and your successes have not made you into a god. You still need to pray, you still need to trust God and you still need to kneel down in His presence!

The choice is yours. You can do it yourself or you can welcome a whole host of agents who are able to make you humble.

Apostle Paul spoke of how a thorn and agent of satan had caused him much distress, much weakness and much infirmity. Indeed, sickness, disease, weakness and need are powerful agents of humility. Paul acknowledged this and considered it to be God's grace towards him. Instead of fighting these agents of humility, he accepted that God had allowed them for his own sake. How terrible and how dangerous pride must be!

God would not allow His precious apostle the privilege of having an abundance of revelation without giving him some associated torment and suffering. Amazingly, it must have been the case that Paul would have been destroyed with pride through the abundance of his revelations. God had to allow a messenger of satan to pummel, irritate, contradict, fight and pound him into a humble state.

So what is a thorn in the flesh? A thorn is a non-specific term for anything that stings, pricks, irritates and causes injury or difficulty. For some people, a thorn in the flesh is their marriage. For others it is their children. Some people's thorn is sickness. Some people's thorn is a situation and a circumstance that does not go away.

Pride is so subtle, so powerful and so pervasive that the most spiritual people are easily destroyed by it. After three years of teaching and training by Jesus, the disciples of Jesus' last argument was about who would be the greatest! Imagine that! Pride is so pervasive that three years of eating humble pie and receiving teachings on humility could not drive away the deadly sin of pride from the apostles. Ooh!

Sickness is a powerful agent of humility. Whether you believe it or not, when you are not well you will start to pray. Many people are humbled by illness and turn to the Lord before they die. Someone once said he felt most people should be struck with a terminal disease because it would humble them greatly. Indeed, it seems the Lord allows many sicknesses because they humble us.

There are two types of politicians: those who have the power and those who want to have power. Those who have the power are often arrogant and are puffed up. The need for power humbles politicians and makes them seem like humble servants who are dying to serve the nation. However, once people are in power and have no need, they change into arrogant men full of themselves and ready to listen to no one.

You will often find people who are blessed of the Lord to have special weaknesses and difficulties that challenge them. It may be a sickness, it may be their marriage or it may be their children. Along with the great anointings and big things come these thorns.

Jesus warned that this would be the mark of His blessing. Jesus promised that His prosperity would come with persecution. Perhaps, the persecution would induce the necessary humility. Along with the promise for great prosperity and wealth, the Lord promised that there would be great problems.

> And Jesus answered and said, Verily I say unto you, there is no man that hath left house, or brethren, or sisters, or father, or mother, or wife, or children, or lands, for my sake, and the gospel's,
>
> But HE SHALL RECEIVE AN HUNDREDFOLD NOW IN THIS TIME, houses, and brethren, and sisters, and mothers, and children, and lands, WITH PERSECUTIONS; and in the world to come eternal life.
>
> Mark 10:29-30

CHAPTER 8

What it Means To Be A Humble Minister Like Jesus Christ

Take my yoke upon you, and learn of me; for I am meek and lowly in heart: and ye shall find rest unto your souls.

Matthew 11:29

One of the main lessons to learn from Jesus Christ is the lesson of humility. Jesus said He was meek and lowly. Jesus advertised His humility. Of all the things we learn from the Lord, perhaps the most important are the lessons of humility.

1. When you are a humble minister like Jesus, you are meek and lowly.

To be a humble pastor is to be meek and lowly. To be lowly means to be modest and to occupy a lower rank. Instead of being loud, noticeable and over-confident, occupy the lower rank and be modest in your appearance and activities. Humility contains a great spiritual power that draws the grace of God.

Some of the greatest and most anointed men of God that I know are the most unassuming men you could ever find. From their physical lowly presentation, you would think they have nothing to offer. Indeed, their lowliness has attracted so much power and grace. Do not be deceived by human patterns and pictures of greatness and importance.

> But when thou art bidden, GO AND SIT DOWN IN THE LOWEST ROOM; that when he that bade thee cometh, he may say unto thee, Friend, go up higher: then shalt thou have worship in the presence of them that sit at meat with thee. For whosoever exalteth himself shall be abased; and he that humbleth himself shall be exalted.
>
> Luke 14:10-11

Follow the Holy Spirit and lead a lowly life of insignificance. Choose the corners which no one likes. Accept the jobs where you will not be seen. Do not advertise all that you are doing. God is the one who needs to see and He can see the lowly better than He can see the high and mighty. When God sees you in the lowly position, He will exalt you Himself. He will exalt you as He has promised.

If you are meek and lowly you will not say:

"I must drive a certain type of car which shows my importance and my greatness."

"I must only wear certain types of clothes."

"My children must go to school with the rich and the famous."

"I must live in a certain area of the city.

"I must have a certain kind of house that shows my greatness and my status in the ministry."

Where do these ideas come from? They come from a spirit of pride of life. The pride that comes from the life that we live on earth is the pride of life. When the spirit of Christ is in you, none of these things will matter. When you are anointed with the spirit of Christ, you will be lowly and you will choose the lower rank. Choose the modest place and do not worry about the lowly impression anyone has about you.

2. When you are a humble minister like Jesus, you do not do what you want.

You do the will and the wishes of the one who sent you. As you become proud you do some of your own will and some of the wishes of your boss.

> For I came down from heaven, NOT TO DO MINE OWN WILL, but the will of him that sent me.
> John 6:38

3. When you are a humble minister like Jesus, you declare that you cannot do anything by yourself.

You need to contact the one who sent you for clarification on almost everything. As you gradually become proud, you do not want people to know that you are actually following someone's instructions.

> Then answered Jesus and said unto them, Verily, verily, I say unto you, THE SON CAN DO NOTHING OF HIMSELF, but what he seeth the Father do: for what things soever he doeth, these also doeth the Son likewise.
> For the Father loveth the Son, and sheweth him all things

that himself doeth: and he will shew him greater works than these, that ye may marvel.

John 5:19-20

4. When you are a humble minister like Jesus, you are happy to let people know that your doctrines and teachings are not original.

You let people know how and where you learnt the many things that you seem to know. Instead of receiving the undeserved praises and admiration of the people, you own up and tell the people that you are simply teaching the things that you have learnt.

He that loveth me not keepeth not my sayings: and THE WORD WHICH YE HEAR IS NOT MINE, but the Father's which sent me.

John 14:24

Jesus answered them, and said, MY DOCTRINE IS NOT MINE, but his that sent me.

John 7:16

5. When you are a humble minister like Jesus, you will tell the people where you get your inspiration from.

You will confess, "It is not my own idea. It is not because I am inspired! It is not because I am self-motivated! I did not come of myself and I do nothing from my own ideas.

If I am anything, it is because of the one who sent me. Pastors do not often speak like this. Associate pastors do not often acknowledge their seniors in such a vivid way. Indeed, most associate pastors want people to think that they as good as their leaders.

Then cried Jesus in the temple as he taught, saying, Ye both know me, and ye know whence I am: and I AM NOT COME OF MYSELF, but he that sent me is true, whom ye know not.

John 7:28

Then said Jesus unto them, when ye have lifted up the Son of man, then shall ye know that I am he, and THAT I DO NOTHING OF MYSELF; but as my Father hath taught me, I speak these things.

And he that sent me is with me: the Father hath not left me alone; for I do always those things that please him.

John 8:28-29

Jesus said unto them, If God were your Father, ye would love me: for I proceeded forth and came from God; NEITHER CAME I OF MYSELF, but he sent me.

John 8:42

Believest thou not that I am in the Father, and the Father in me? the words that I speak unto you I SPEAK NOT OF MYSELF: but the Father that dwelleth in me, he doeth the works.

John 14:10

6. When you are a humble minister like Jesus, you will be obedient in every area.

And being found in fashion as a man, he HUMBLED HIMSELF, and BECAME OBEDIENT unto death, even the death of the cross.

Philippians 2:8

Remember that being obedient is being like Jesus and being like Jesus is being humble! Obedience is a real sign of real humility.

Please read the scripture above. Because Jesus was humble He became obedient even to the death of the cross. Obedience is a sign of real humility because you set aside your "mind". You set aside your own thinking. You accept that your thoughts and ideas are irrelevant and immaterial.

When you are proud you cannot easily set aside your own ideas and thoughts. Many pastors struggle with pride in their own marriages. You see, in marriage, some wives do not easily accept that their thoughts and ideas are irrelevant and immaterial. Indeed, they think the opposite. They think that their ideas and their thoughts are very important and relevant to decisions being taken. Because of this, many wives are not obedient to their husbands. Simply put, they are not obedient to their husbands because they are too proud to set aside their thoughts, ideas and plans.

When the pastor goes to the church, he meets people he can easily direct and instruct. He gives them ideas, instructions, and wisdom. Congregants set aside their own thoughts and ideas and wholeheartedly swallow the wisdom coming from the pastor. Why is this? Because the congregants behave humbly towards their pastors.

But these same congregants are not likely to behave humbly towards their husbands. The ugly devil of pride rears itself in marriages and destroys the happiness, the peace and the tranquillity of ministers' marriages.

7. **When you are a humble minister like Jesus, you will do any low profile job.**

Ye call me Master and Lord: and ye say well; for so I am. If I then, your Lord and Master, have washed your feet; ye also ought to wash one another's feet.
John 13:13-14

Washing feet represents all the low profile jobs in the kingdom of God. To wash feet is to do the lowest and dirtiest job in relation to another. Many times Christians aim for lofty roles and high-sounding positions. I am the "Officer for washing feet"! That does not sound like a very glamorous position. Most of us would prefer to say "I am the minister in charge. I am the senior pastor. I am the provost. I am the rector. I am the Bishop. I am the head pastor. I am a spiritual father. I am an Elder."

Most ministers want to do only high profile jobs. What about the low profile jobs? People want to write books for Americans and other rich Christians. Perhaps you should try writing a book that your poor church members would understand. Stop aiming for high-sounding roles and take up low ranking jobs in the kingdom. Do all the low profile jobs that God gives to you. That is a sign of humility in the kingdom.

8. When you are a humble minister like Jesus, you will not compete with other ministers.

> Then there arose a reasoning among them, which of them should be greatest.
>
> Luke 9:46

The disciples were not just content with being great. *They wanted to be great in comparison to the other disciples.* Therefore, they wanted to be the greatest.

To become competitive is to seek to be great in comparison to others. Most of the wrong things we do in ministry have their roots in "comparison". Where does he live? Where do his children go to school? What car does he drive? Is his car nicer than mine? Is his house nicer than mine?

Competition extends into spiritual things as well. Is his church bigger than mine? Does he have more miracles than me? Are his crowds larger than mine?

You are not just content with having large crowds. You want crowds that are larger than your friend's crowds.

Humility accepts the lower rank. When you are a humble pastor, you will not even lift up your eyes to compare what you have with another. You will say to yourself, "He is greater and I know it. I thank God for what He is doing in my brother's life."

9. When you are a humble minister like Jesus, you accept to be the younger.

> But ye shall not be so: but he that is greatest among you, let him be AS THE YOUNGER; and he that is chief, as he that doth serve.
>
> Luke 22:26

David was the youngest in his house. What did that mean for him? It meant that he was not chosen for important jobs. It also meant that he was not selected to do important things. You must remember that when Samuel came on the scene to anoint one of the children of Jesse, David was not even counted or chosen by the family. In fact, he was not even remembered.

To be a humble pastor is to accept to be the younger and the youngest. When I became a pastor, several people disdained me and spoke disparagingly about me. For most people, I was a "small boy". I was too young, too small and too insignificant to be anything in the ministry. They would ask, "Who is Dag? Where did he come from? What does he know?"

For years, I resented the references to me as a "small boy". Indeed, I always calculated my age in relation to theirs. I always insisted that I was not that much younger than anyone.

Today, I am glad that I am the younger. I accept that I am the younger. It is good for me to be the younger. I am nothing and nobody. I found out that it was a blessing to be the youngest. You must learn to take that position and assume that your opinion does not matter because you are the younger.

In my position as the younger, no one ever appointed me. No one ever chose me for any important job. I was never selected to be class prefect, school prefect, Scripture Union President or Fellowship leader. But it is still a blessing to be the younger. It is a humble position.

Recently, some reporters were interviewing me and wanted my opinion. In my surprise, I almost blurted out, "Why do you want my opinion? I am nobody." But I managed to mutter a few words and escape from their microphones. Indeed, I had gotten used to being the younger, never being counted, never being called and never being chosen. If you accept to be the younger and defer to others you will bring upon yourself the blessings that only spiritual people experience. Do not be worried that no one chooses you. God will choose you Himself.

CHAPTER 9

What It Means To Be Puffed Up

Now SOME ARE PUFFED UP, as though I would not come to you. But I will come to you shortly, if the Lord will, and will know, NOT THE SPEECH OF THEM WHICH ARE PUFFED UP, but the power.

1 Corinthians 4:18-19

It is reported commonly that there is fornication among you, and such fornication as is not so much as named among the Gentiles, that one should have his father's wife. And YE ARE PUFFED UP, AND HAVE NOT RATHER MOURNED, that he that hath done this deed might be taken away from among you.

1 Corinthians 5:1-2

Let no one cheat you of your reward, taking delight in false humility and worship of angels, intruding into those things which he has not seen, VAINLY PUFFED UP BY HIS FLESHLY MIND.

Colossians 2:18 NKJV

The swelling of pride is the cardinal symptom of a deep-seated evil condition. Unfortunately, it is not easy to see when a person is puffed up. It is even more difficult to see when you are puffed up yourself. Here is what it means to be puffed up.

To be puffed up is to be swollen! To be puffed up is to think you are very important! To be puffed up is to be arrogant! To be puffed up is to be pompous! To be puffed up is to be full of yourself! To be puffed up is to be high and mighty! To be puffed up is to be haughty and conceited! To be puffed up is to be boastful! To be puffed up is to feel superior! To be puffed up is to be snobbish!

To be puffed up is to be swollen with pride. This puffing up speaks of a spiritual condition. This deadly spiritual state mimics the equally dangerous physical condition of your body being swollen. When the physical body is swollen, you usually have some dangerous illness like a kidney disease, a liver disease or even a heart condition. A person with a swollen face, swollen abdomen and swollen feet is ill! Such a person may even be near to death. All measures are taken to reduce the swelling because the swelling is a great symptom of danger.

This is what it is like to be puffed up spiritually. In the natural, when a person is puffed up, he is filled with water. When a person is puffed up spiritually, he is filled with pride, not water.

When a person is filled with water, it is because he has a disease in his kidney, liver or heart. When a person is puffed up and filled with pride, it is because he has a spiritual disease in his soul, his mind and his heart. He may be filled with delusions that are destroying his heart.

Truly Great Or Puffed Up?

In the natural, a person could be a large or tall size. To be a large or extra large person is not the same as being ill. It is when a person is abnormally swollen with fluid or fat that his size becomes a symptom of disease. A person who is large or extra large in size has grown slowly and normally into that dimension. A person who is puffed up or swollen grew rapidly and abnormally into that state.

Watch out for people who suddenly develop evil attitudes because of recent promotion and elevation! Natural growth is slow and almost unnoticeable. Dangerous and evil swellings appear suddenly! You may wake up in the morning and find your face swollen. You may wake up in the morning and find your feet swollen. That is not the same as the natural growth of your feet.

Pride and arrogance often come to those who suddenly become wealthy, successful and great. You often wonder why they have developed these attitudes. This is why God often allows us to suffer and rise slowly into great heights. A rapid elevation is often not a good thing for a human being. It is this swelling that leads to a fall.

How Can You Avoid Being Puffed Up?

You can avoid being puffed up by learning about all those who were puffed up in the bible. These examples teach us all about arrogance and pride. Pride always comes before a fall and each of these characters we will study fell dramatically. The falls of these bible characters have been recorded for us to learn from. This is not a book I am writing to you. It is a book I am writing to us all. If I was in heaven I would be writing to you but because I am on earth I am writing a message that affects us all.

I want you to study the stories and testimonies of the well-known cases of pride and arrogance. These characters have played out most of the features we need to know about. History is just waiting to be repeated in your life if you allow it. The lives of Lucifer, Vashti, Nebuchadnezzar, Belshazzar, Rehoboam and Korah are before us all for our learning and our safety.

CHAPTER 10

What It Means To Be Puffed Up Like Lucifer

Now SOME ARE PUFFED UP, as though I would not come to you. But I will come to you shortly, if the Lord will, and will know, NOT THE SPEECH OF THEM WHICH ARE PUFFED UP, but the power.

1 Corinthians 4:18-19

Lucifer is the first and best example of someone who was puffed up, swollen with pride, arrogance and delusions. People who become puffed up and swollen with pride are following the example of Lucifer. So how did Lucifer become puffed up?

1. You can be puffed up like Lucifer when you have unholy and evil ambitions.

Exalting yourself like Lucifer is to aim for greatness that God has not given you. Lucifer was puffed up because he had unholy, ungodly and evil ambitions for greatness.

This evil ambition of satan is exposed clearly through the words of Lucifer: I will ascend into…! I will ascend above…! I will exalt…! I will sit also …! I will be like …!

> For thou hast said in thine heart, I WILL ASCEND into heaven, I WILL EXALT my throne above the stars of God: I WILL SIT ALSO upon the mount of the congregation, in the sides of the north: I WILL ASCEND above the heights of the clouds; I WILL BE LIKE the most High.
> Isaiah 14:13-14

I remember being corrected by a Jewish man. He pointed out to me that I should not use such words like *"I am", "I will", "I can", "I have" and "I will not"*. He explained to me that it is only God who can say, *"I am", "I will", "I can", "I will not" and "I have"*. I realized that he was right. I felt ashamed of myself because I had known how Lucifer had used such language to express his evil ambitions.

What ambitions do you have? Do you want to be great? Do you want to have lots of money? Do you want to be a powerful rich man? Do you want to be a famous man of God? Do you want to be a senior pastor of your church? Do you want to move out of the position of an assistant and become the senior pastor? Do you want to become your boss? Do you want to become the wife of your boss? Do you want to replace your pastor's wife? Do you want to become the first lady? Do you want to be the girlfriend of that famous soccer player?

If these ambitions are not God given and God ordained, they are evil and they will get you into big trouble. Everyone has secret ambitions and unvoiced goals. What dreams do you have? You must always watch your heart! Your visions and dreams reveal your heart. When satan gives you visions and dreams, you will be a man filled with wrong evil ambitions. These wrong ambitions are what show that you are filled with arrogance and pride. These evil ambitions will make you fight and struggle for supremacy. You can be dangerously puffed up because of your demonic ambitions.

2. **You can be puffed up like Lucifer when you forget why and how you were appointed.**

   Thou art the anointed cherub that covereth; and I HAVE SET THEE SO: thou wast upon the holy mountain of God; thou hast walked up and down in the midst of the stones of fire.
   Ezekiel 28:14

   Once you have been appointed into a position, you must maintain a certain level of humility. Every position that you occupy is an appointment from God. Sometimes it is an appointment from other human beings. These realities must make us humble. One of the signs of pride is seen in people who forget that they were appointed or set into their positions.

   Sometimes, someone is appointed as a pastor but he quickly forgets how he was favoured and elevated to occupy that position of honour. Indeed, the pride and rudeness exhibited by appointed officers reveals how people have forgotten that they were appointed and can be removed!

3. **You can be puffed up like Lucifer when you forget why and how you were created.**

   Thou wast perfect in thy ways from the day that THOU WAST CREATED, till iniquity was found in thee.
   Ezekiel 28:15

Satan soon forgot that he was a created being and that is why he wanted to rise and replace God on his throne. Perhaps his singing and music attracted so much praise that he thought the music came from within himself. Do not forget that you are created! That means you are a normal human being! Just accepting that you are normal shows that you are not puffed up.

Accept that you need to eat!
Accept that you need to drink water!
Accept that you need to take medicine!
Accept that you need to have sex!
Accept that you need to marry!
Accept that you want to have children! Accept that you are just like everyone else.

Accept the fact that you need help. That is what it means to be humble.

Many people do not like to discuss realities! They feel that certain things are indecent and unclean. When you speak about sex or marriage they look at you as though you are vulgar or profane. Dear friend, it is humility to accept your human needs, desires and tendencies. It is wise and humble to understand yourself and to accept yourself. This will not harm you. When you humble yourself you will be elevated. When you are puffed up and cannot bring yourself to behold or discuss your human realities, you will find yourself falling.

Some people who decided that they were above marriage and above the sexual activities of normal marriage have actually fallen far below the natural created state and into depraved forms of sexuality. By avoiding the normal relationships with women, some have fallen into depraved conditions of having sex with their own sex or with little children.

Some people, who would not want to discuss marriage or sex, end up having numerous illicit secret sexual relations. Such people will secretly give themselves over to pornography and other perversions.

To accept your humanity is to avoid embarrassment and humiliation. To accept that you need to have sex is to agree that you are normal and not special. To think that you are special and do not need to do the base activities that other human beings do, is to be puffed up.

It is like building a house without a toilet and saying, "I do not need a toilet. I am above such base and smelly activities." Do not be puffed up! Accept that you are a man like every other man and a woman like every other woman. Take decisions that reveal that you respect these realities. That is humility. Do not be like Lucifer who forgot that he was created.

4. Lucifer was puffed up because he fell from his position.

> By the multitude of thy merchandise they have filled the midst of thee with violence, and thou hast sinned: therefore I WILL CAST THEE AS PROFANE OUT OF THE MOUNTAIN OF GOD: and I WILL DESTROY
>
> Ezekiel 28:16

One of the reasons why we know that Lucifer was puffed up is because he fell from his lofty position! Pride comes before a fall! Therefore, a fall is a symptom and a sign that pride is nearby.

1. Lucifer was cast out of the mountain. In other words, he was dismissed and he lost his position. People who lose their positions often suffer from pride.

2. Lucifer was destroyed. In other words, all that he was doing was brought to nothing. His life and ministry were destroyed. People whose lives, careers, businesses and ministries are destroyed often suffer from some form of pride.

3. A fire came out from within Lucifer and devoured him. This shows that Lucifer was destroyed from internal forces and not external forces. Churches, companies, businesses, political parties that are destroyed are often destroyed from within.

Thou hast defiled thy sanctuaries by the multitude of thine iniquities, by the iniquity of thy traffick; therefore will I BRING FORTH A FIRE FROM THE MIDST OF THEE, IT SHALL DEVOUR THEE, and I will bring thee to ashes upon the earth in the sight of all them that behold thee.

All they that know thee among the people shall be astonished at thee: thou shalt be a terror, and NEVER SHALT THOU BE ANY MORE.

Ezekiel 28:18-19

CHAPTER 11

What It Means To Be Puffed Up Like Vashti

Let no one cheat you of your reward, taking delight in false humility and worship of angels, intruding into those things which he has not seen, VAINLY PUFFED UP BY HIS FLESHLY MIND.

        Colossians 2:18, NKJV

1. You are puffed up like Vashti when you no longer obey your husband!

> What shall we do unto the queen Vashti according to law, because she hath not performed the commandment of the king Ahasuerus by the chamberlains?
>
> Esther 1:15

Vashti is a well-known woman of pride. She was too big to obey her husband. As the scripture predicts, she fell from her high position of being the First Lady. Vashti was never heard of again. Is that what you want to happen to you? How do you know that you are a proud woman? We cannot say that you are humble because of what you say about yourself. But we can say that you are proud if your life follows the example of Vashti. Vashti did not obey her husband. Not obeying a husband is a sign that you are like Vashti and therefore it is a sign that you are proud.

I sent a missionary to a foreign country. When he married his wife, she was a nice, sweet, obedient little girl. Through the blessings of God, she gave birth to a number of children. Finally, when her womb was full she declared, "I will not go to the mission field any more. I have had enough. I am fed up. It is over."

She told her husband, "I am not coming."

Then she told the mission director, "I will never go back to the mission field. I have had enough. My husband should follow me! I will not follow him any more!"

This young lady had now grown wings and had become too big and too resistant to obey her husband. She had enjoyed the married status for some time and was not so impressed! She had also given birth to the children that she wanted. Who was this young man to tell her what to do and where to live? She simply disobeyed her husband and went her own way.

This is a good example of pride. This young lady would not have behaved like this some years earlier. She would have pledged her obedience to the mission and to the ministry of her husband. Becoming puffed up is to experience a rapid swelling. Being puffed up is when a person quickly develops a state of pride.

2. **You are puffed up like Vashti when you are hard, resistant and unyielding!**

> On the seventh day, when the heart of the king was merry with wine, he commanded Mehuman, Biztha, Harbona, Bigtha, and Abagtha, Zethar, and Carcas, the seven chamberlains that served in the presence of Ahasuerus the king, To bring Vashti the queen before the king with the crown royal, to shew the people and the princes her beauty: for she was fair to look on.
> BUT THE QUEEN VASHTI REFUSED TO COME AT THE KING'S COMMANDMENT by his chamberlains: therefore was the king very wroth, and his anger burned in him.
>
> Esther 1:10-12

Vashti was hard, stubborn and unyielding. All her advisers failed to persuade her. She had a strong opinion and no one could change her mind. The queen refused to come. Perhaps, when the king first chose her to be his queen she came running, willing to do anything and everything. But today, she could not be moved! Watch out for those hardened resistant women with the spirit of Vashti.

Your hardness, your stubbornness, your resistance and your refusal to bend are clear signs of pride. That is what makes you a modern day Vashti.

A proud person never says "Yes" when "Yes" is the right answer. A proud person never says "No" when "No" is the right answer. A woman who never bends, never yields, is never gracious, never flows and never agrees, is just another proud Vashti.

How is it that you can never change your mind? What is the use of a mind if it cannot be changed? Indeed, you may say, "Who am I? I am nothing. I am a humble servant of God. I am the Lord's handmaiden. I am an ant before the Lord." But your stubbornness and resistance to change reveals that you are actually proud and puffed up. You say nice things about yourself. You declare humility. You proclaim your goodness and call yourself a daughter of destiny. But you are just like Vashti who could not be moved around by her husband.

3. We know Vashti was puffed up because she fell from her position and was set aside.

All the evidence you need to confirm the fact that Vashti was proud is found in the fact that she was set aside. To be set aside, to be dismissed and to be replaced is a result of pride. Pride comes before a fall. Resistance, disobedience and stubbornness were the things that brought about the fall of Vashti. Are you hard? Are you stubborn? Do people say you are stubborn, hard and resistant? Do people find you to be someone who does not change her mind? Then that is not a compliment. That is a dangerous sign.

Watch out! You are likely to be replaced or exchanged for someone very soon. There is hardly any downward move that does not come from pride.

In my experience as an employer, I have found that those resistant to change almost always lose their position. I notice how stubborn people are replaced with softer, yielding and ready-to-learn personalities.

In politics, it is when a government becomes proud and resistant to change that it ends up being replaced by a more humble and listening party. People who are not open to new ideas are often replaced by people who are willing to learn something new.

If it please the king, let there go a royal commandment from him, and let it be written among the laws of the

Persians and the Medes, that it be not altered, That Vashti come no more before king Ahasuerus; and LET THE KING GIVE HER ROYAL ESTATE UNTO ANOTHER THAT IS BETTER THAN SHE.

And when the king's decree which he shall make shall be published throughout all his empire, (for it is great,) all the wives shall give to their husbands honour, both to great and small.

And the saying pleased the king and the princes; and the king did according to the word of Memucan:

Esther 1:19-21

Then said the king's servants that ministered unto him, Let there be fair young virgins sought for the king:

And let the king appoint officers in all the provinces of his kingdom, that they may gather together all the fair young virgins unto Shushan the palace, to the house of the women, unto the custody of Hege the king's chamberlain, keeper of the women; and let their things for purification be given them:

AND LET THE MAIDEN WHICH PLEASETH THE KING BE QUEEN INSTEAD OF VASHTI.

And the thing pleased the king; and he did so.

Esther 2:2-4

And the king loved Esther above all the women, and she obtained grace and favour in his sight more than all the virgins; so that he set the royal crown upon her head, and MADE HER QUEEN INSTEAD OF VASHTI.

Esther 2:17

CHAPTER 12

What It Means To Be Puffed Up Like Nebuchadnezzar

Now **SOME ARE PUFFED UP**, as though I would not come to you. But I will come to you shortly, if the Lord will, and will know, **NOT THE SPEECH OF THEM WHICH ARE PUFFED UP**, but the power.

1 Corinthians 4:18-19

1. You are puffed up like Nebuchadnezzar when you do not listen to warnings from the pastors and the prophets.

Nebuchadnezzar was warned by the prophet to humble himself before the Lord. God speaks to men through his servants the prophets, the pastors and the teachers. Men often disregard and manhandle the servants of the Lord who speak for Him.

Nebuchadnezzar was warned by the prophet Daniel. He refused to listen and he paid the price for that. The price he paid was to have a mental illness for seven years. It was only by the mercy of God that He was not totally removed from office.

I have often wondered as politicians lambasted pastors for speaking the truth. The politicians wanted the ministers of the gospel to tow their line and say things that would favour their cause. They wanted the pastors to promote their party. If you do not heed to the voice of the pastor, you may pay a heavy price.

I once met a rich man in a public place. I told him, "You must be born again." I don't know why I told him that he had to be born again. I guessed that I sensed the need for this man to repent. This man was so incensed by my message to him. He got angry and shouted at me in front of everyone. My counsel was not acceptable to him. This is what Daniel begged from Nebuchadnezzar, "Please let my counsel be acceptable unto you."

> Wherefore, O KING, LET MY COUNSEL BE ACCEPTABLE UNTO THEE, and break off thy sins by righteousness, and thine iniquities by shewing mercy to the poor; if it may be a lengthening of thy tranquillity.
>
> Daniel 4:27

Because this rich man had created such a scene, I decided to say nothing further. He was someone I hardly knew and I knew I would not see much of him anymore. I did meet him again in about three months. This time, however, I said nothing to him. I mumbled a civil greeting and moved on.

A few weeks later, I got a message that this man wanted to see me. I wondered why this person would want to see me of all people. Apparently, he had been taken ill and was in hospital. As his condition worsened, I got another urgent call. But before I was able to see him, he passed away.

I spoke to someone who saw him die. This rich man died a frightening death as he passed into the arms of waiting evil spirits. Indeed, he did not die the death of a righteous man. As the rich man hung in the balance between life and death, his confidence, his boldness and his strength were taken away. He was gripped with fright as he saw the demons and evil spirits gathering around to take him away into outer darkness.

He died shrieking and crying, "Can you see them? They are coming for me!" He would grab the people standing around his bed and say, "Can't you see them? They are coming for me!"

Dear friend, you may laugh and mock when the pastor speaks but a day will come when you will not laugh. Pastors and prophets are messengers of God. You must be careful about what you say to pastors. You must be careful about how you handle their words!

2. **You are puffed up like Nebuchadnezzar when you think that your achievements have been by your own efforts.**

> The king spake, and said, is not this great Babylon, that I have built for the house of the kingdom by the might of my power, and for the honour of my majesty?
>
> Daniel 4:30

You must watch yourself in case you think you have achieved what you have achieved by your own strength and ability. It is by the grace of God that you have what you have! We know that Nebuchadnezzar was puffed up and proud because of the things he said. He ascribed the greatness of the city, Babylon, to his wisdom and abilities. He should have acknowledged God and declared that he had built Babylon by the grace of God.

There was a man who was trapped in a building after an earthquake. After three days and nights he was rescued and taken to the hospital. He was interviewed by the news media. Everyone wanted to know about the ordeal he had been through.

"How did you survive under the rubble for three days and nights?"

The man answered, "I am a man of strong will power. I am a determined person. I always do what I have decided to do and I stick to my vision and I maintain my purpose at all times."

"Wow," the reporter said, "That's great. Congratulations on your great achievement."

The reporter also interviewed his wife. He was stunned to have almost the same response from the wife.

"How do you feel about what happened? How was your husband able to survive his ordeal underground for so long?"

His wife answered, "My husband is a man of strong willpower. He is very focussed and determined. When he sets his mind on something he usually achieves it. I have been married to him for twenty-five years. I know my husband and I think that is why he survived for so long. He is a survivor," she smiled. The reporter then interviewed the doctors who were looking after the man.

"I am sure you were amazed to find this man alive after so long." The doctors concurred, "Our patient is resilient. He is a man of strong willpower, very determined and very focussed. We think he was determined not to die and that is why he survived the ordeal."

A week later, this man with the strong willpower had a heart attack and died suddenly. It seems his will power was unable to sustain him. The question I ask is, "Where was his strong will power? Seven days after the earthquake, where was his strong will power and determination?

Instead of giving glory to God, these people were ascribing the miracle of life to resilience, strong will power and determination. God does not like it when you boast about things that He has given you as though you did not receive them.

What hast thou that thou didst not receive? If thou didst receive it then why dost thou boast as though thou didst not receive it? (1 Corinthians 4:7).

3. We know Nebuchadnezzar was puffed up because he fell from his position and dwelled with the beasts of the field.

The prophecy of Nebuchadnezzar's judgment was fulfilled in one stroke. Pride always comes before a fall. The illness of Nebuchadnezzar was to help him recognize the greatness of God in his life. I read a book in which a man claimed to have gone to heaven and met with saints who had passed on to heaven. He met a great pastor who had had a great ministry on earth. This pastor explained to him that he had become proud whilst on earth. He then told him that the Lord had given him a humbling sickness through which he had eventually died. When he arrived in heaven, he realised that the humbling sickness was the grace of God to his life. Through that illness he had repented and humbled himself just before he died. He then said something even more alarming to the prophet who was having the vision.

He said, "When I got to heaven, I began to pray that the Lord would give many of my followers the same humbling illness so that they would repent before they came here. As I thought over this vision, my heart was broken. I realised that many of us suffer so much from pride that we need such external forces to break us down. Notice how this happened in the life of Nebuchadnezzar:

> At the end of twelve months he walked in the palace of the kingdom of Babylon. The king spake, and said, Is not this great Babylon, that I have built for the house of the kingdom by the might of my power, and for the honour of my majesty?
> WHILE THE WORD WAS IN THE KING'S MOUTH, THERE FELL A VOICE FROM HEAVEN, SAYING, O KING NEBUCHADNEZZAR, TO THEE IT IS SPOKEN; THE KINGDOM IS DEPARTED FROM THEE.
> And they shall drive thee from men, and thy dwelling shall be with the beasts of the field: they shall make thee to eat

grass as oxen, and seven times shall pass over thee, until thou know that the most High ruleth in the kingdom of men, and giveth it to whomsoever he will.

The same hour was the thing fulfilled upon Nebuchadnezzar: and he was driven from men, and did eat grass as oxen, and his body was wet with the dew of heaven, till his hairs were grown like eagles 'feathers, and his nails like birds' claws.

Daniel 4:29-33

CHAPTER 13

What It Means To Be Puffed Up Like Belshazzar

It is reported commonly that there is fornication among you, and such fornication as is not so much as named among the Gentiles, that one should have his father's wife. And YE ARE PUFFED UP, AND HAVE NOT RATHER MOURNED, that he that hath done this deed might be taken away from among you.

1 Corinthians 5:1-2

1. You are puffed up like Belshazzar when you do not respect the church nor the pastors.

Belshazzar drank wine from the vessels in the temple. He was having a party and praising the gods of gold and silver. Often, unbelievers have fun and manifest their lusts and passions without restraint. This is exactly what Belshazzar was doing.

However, there was no need for Belshazzar to despise God at his party. But in the midst of the party, he had an idea. He did not want to drink from an ordinary glass. He wanted to drink from the church's cups and vessels. He had cups and he had glasses but he wanted to make fun of the church and God's people. You must be careful when you lose respect for the church of God and its ministers.

One Sunday I was invited to preach in a church which was situated in a well developed, prosperous neighbourhood. That church did not have enough parking space and the members would park along the street. One church member parked in front of a certain rich man's house. This rich man was so incensed when someone parked his car in front of his house. He came out of the house swearing, cursing and hurling angry insults at the church member and the entire church. He forced the church member to remove his car from the road in front of his house.

As he turned and walked back into his house he fell down and died on the pavement. He did not even get to his gate.

You must be careful when you shout at the church members and insult the church and its pastors. That very Sunday evening, canopies went up in preparation for the funeral in the house. Belshazzar insulted the church when he used the cups and wine from the temple. That very night the handwriting appeared on the wall and he ceased to exist.

> Belshazzar, whiles he tasted the wine, commanded to bring the golden and silver vessels which his father Nebuchadnezzar had taken out of the temple which was in Jerusalem; that the king, and his princes, his wives, and his

concubines, might drink therein. Then THEY BROUGHT THE GOLDEN VESSELS THAT WERE TAKEN OUT OF THE TEMPLE OF THE HOUSE OF GOD which was at Jerusalem; and the king, and his princes, his wives, and his concubines, DRANK IN THEM.

Daniel 5:2-3

2. You are puffed up like Belshazzar when you think that God is not important and that the only things that were important are gold, silver and wood.

They drank wine, and PRAISED THE GODS OF GOLD, and OF SILVER, of BRASS, of IRON, of WOOD, and of STONE.

Daniel 5:4

You are deceived and proud when you think that the only important thing in this world is money. Many people consider their power to come from the money they have. I once met a rich young man who was full of insults for God and for pastors. One day, after a short interaction with a pastor, he started shouting at the pastor.

He shouted, "What do you have?" He continued shouting, "I have everything. What do you have that I do not have? I have everything!"

I listened as this man hurled insults at the pastor, all the while shouting, "I have everything, what do you have?" Somehow, he calculated his worth by what he had. Just like Belshazzar, he praised the gods of gold, of silver, of wood and of stone. In other words he had confidence in gold, in silver and in his house of stone and wood.

Dear friend, is that what your confidence lies in? Silver, gold, wood and stone? Are you just like Belshazzar? You are puffed up when your confidence is in your money. It will rot before your eyes and its power to save you will not work.

3. **Belshazzar was puffed up because he did not learn from his father's mistakes.**

> O thou king, the most high GOD GAVE NEBUCHADNEZZAR THY FATHER a kingdom, and majesty, and glory, and honour:. . .
> AND THOU HIS SON, O Belshazzar, hast not humbled thine heart, though thou knewest all this;
> But hast lifted up thyself against the Lord of heaven; and they have brought the vessels of his house before thee, and thou, and thy lords, thy wives, and thy concubines, have drunk wine in them; and thou hast praised the gods of silver, and gold, of brass, iron, wood, and stone, which see not, nor hear, nor know: and the God in whose hand thy breath is, and whose are all thy ways, hast thou not glorified:
> Daniel 5:18, 22-23

Belshazzar should have learnt some lessons from the mistakes of his father Nebuchadnezzar. When sons are filled with pride, they do not learn from their fathers. They criticize them! They mock them! They turn away from them! They despise them! This is a great mistake because they fail to learn anything from their fathers.

We know Belshazzar was proud because he fell from his lofty position. He was killed and became a dead body that night. He turned into worm infested rotting flesh that night because he did not learn anything from his own father. He did not learn any lessons from what had happened to his own father. Handwriting appeared on the wall and that was the end of this puffed up son of Nebuchadnezzar.

CHAPTER 14

What It Means To Be Puffed Up Like Rehoboam

Now SOME ARE PUFFED UP, as though I would not come to you. But I will come to you shortly, if the Lord will, and will know, NOT THE SPEECH OF THEM WHICH ARE PUFFED UP, but the power.

1 Corinthians 4:18-19

1. **You are puffed up like Rehoboam, when as a newly appointed ruler, you do not respect the elders.**

You shall rise before the grayheaded and honor the aged, and you shall revere your God; I am the Lord.
                                        Leviticus 19:32 (NASB)

And the king answered the people roughly, and forsook the old men's counsel that they gave him;
                                        1 Kings 12:13

Rehoboam the newly appointed king, in his arrogance, despised the input of the older advisers.

It is important to respect and regard people who are older and more experienced than you are. Why is this? A younger person learns principles and theories about how things are supposed to work. Based on the theories and ideologies, things are supposed to go a certain way. Indeed, there seems to be no reason why things should not go a certain way. But in real life, things do not work out according to the principles and the theories we are taught. Why is that?

The human being introduces the human factor that modifies the outcome of things. The human factor causes life to be governed by human traits of selfishness, greed, lust, wickedness, laziness, betrayal and jealousy. Most theories are set aside by these negative human traits.

An experienced person is someone who knows what will happen in real life because he has seen the negative human traits play out to the full. His opinion is therefore important because he will tell you about the surprising twists and turns you must expect because of negative human traits.

Almost every human government sets out to do good. They come in with slogans like, *"A better nation"*, *"Yes we can"*, *"Positive change"*, *"We are moving forward"*. Unfortunately, most of these goals are never achieved because things do not turn out according to the theories. The wickedness, the jealousies, the lusts, the greed and the selfishness of mankind change everything. This is where old age and experience come in. It is pride and arrogance to despise the input God brings to you through old and experienced persons. They may not know many of the modern things but they know how human nature works. They know exactly what is going to happen in the future because they have seen it all before.

2. **You are puffed up like Rehoboam when you have no regard for the advice from a new source.**

> And king Rehoboam consulted with the old men, that stood before Solomon his father while he yet lived, and said, How do ye advise that I may answer this people?
> And they spake unto him, saying, If thou wilt be a servant unto this people this day, and wilt serve them, and answer them, and speak good words to them, then they will be thy servants for ever.
> But he forsook the counsel of the old men, which they had given him, and consulted with the young men that were grown up with him, and which stood before him:
> 1 Kings 12:6-8

Another symptom of pride is the rejection of advice that comes from any new or unknown source. Pride always comes before a fall. Many of us would have been promoted if we were humble enough to receive input, guidance and help from new and unknown sources. Rehoboam was not used to these old men. He was familiar with the younger group of people and in arrogance he rejected the input from those he considered to be strangers.

3. **Rehoboam was puffed up because he issued threats and insults soon after his appointment.**

> And spake to them after the counsel of the young men, saying, My father made your yoke heavy, and I will add to your yoke: my father also chastised you with whips, but I will chastise you with scorpions.
> 1 Kings 12:13-14

Watch out for those who threaten people all the time. "I will kill you", "I will show you where power lies", "Do you know who I am?", "Don't mess with me". It is only when you feel big, powerful and invincible that you threaten others.

You may think in your heart, "I am great and there is no one who can stand before me". But that is not so. God is greater than you and God rules in the affairs of men!

I remember a certain country that had a revolution. The revolutionary leader did many amazing things in the country. He closed down universities, he burnt down markets, he arrested people at will and executed those he thought were guilty. One day, he made an announcement in public. He said, "I am going to turn my attention to the churches." That was the beginning of a new wave of pressure and persecution against the church.

But I also noticed that it was the beginning of the decline of that revolutionary government. From that time onwards, the popularity and the power of the government dwindled. The revolutionary government was forced to metamorphose into a democratic government and give up all its autocratic powers.

The Holy Spirit prompted me to notice this decline in the government's authority and power. You must be careful when you touch the church. Belshazzar was having a great time. He could have continued having a great time without tampering with the church. Watch out for people who think the church is a weak and easy victim. Many have threatened the church over the centuries. Nothing has become of these people. They have all perished and the church has grown stronger and stronger!

4. Rehoboam was puffed up because he fell from his position as the ruler of all the tribes of Israel to become the ruler of only Judah.

So when all Israel saw that the king hearkened not unto them, the people answered the king, saying, What portion have we in David? neither have we inheritance in the son of Jesse: to your tents, O Israel: now see to thine own

house, David. So Israel departed unto their tents. But as for the children of Israel which dwelt in the cities of Judah, Rehoboam reigned over them...
So Israel rebelled against the house of David unto this day. And it came to pass, when all Israel heard that Jeroboam was come again, that they sent and called him unto the congregation, and made him king over all Israel: THERE WAS NONE THAT FOLLOWED THE HOUSE OF DAVID, BUT THE TRIBE OF JUDAH ONLY
1 Kings 12:16-17, 19-20

Rehoboam inherited a large and powerful kingdom made up of twelve tribes. He also inherited all the riches of Solomon. And yet, by the first cabinet meeting he had lost control of the majority of the country. Also, within five years he lost all the wealth that he inherited from his father. King Shishak, the king of Egypt came and took away all the wealth to Egypt. Rehoboam was forced to replace all the gold in the temple with brass.

And it came to pass, that in THE FIFTH YEAR of king Rehoboam Shishak king of Egypt came up against Jerusalem, because they had transgressed against the Lord...
So Shishak king of Egypt came up against Jerusalem, AND TOOK AWAY THE TREASURES OF THE HOUSE OF THE LORD, AND THE TREASURES OF THE KING'S HOUSE; he took all: he carried away also the shields of gold which Solomon had made.
Instead of which king Rehoboam made shields of brass, and committed them to the hands of the chief of the guard, that kept the entrance of the king's house.
2 Chronicles 12:2, 9-10

Rehoboam fell from being one of the richest kings in the world to become one of the poorest. This fall was due to pride. Companies fall from being the number one in their field because of pride. Great nations are reduced to nothing because of their pride.

CHAPTER 15

What It Means To Be Puffed Up Like Pharaoh

> Now SOME ARE PUFFED UP, as though I would not come to you. But I will come to you shortly, if the Lord will, and will know, NOT THE SPEECH OF THEM WHICH ARE PUFFED UP, but the power.
>
> 1 Corinthians 4:18-19

Pharaoh was puffed up! Pharaoh was full of himself! Pharaoh is the quintessential arrogant authority figure who does not know that his power comes from the Lord. Pharaoh made a series of mistakes that are repeated today by people who are in authority. Let us go through the series of mistakes that you can make because of your arrogance.

1. **You are puffed up like Pharaoh when you are over-confident.**

Your over confidence will make you refuse to consider other options for your future. Pharaoh had no doubts in his mind that he could deal with the Israelites.

Pharaoh did not recognize a change in season and or a change in his strength. Many heads of state in Africa were offered options of leaving their countries and living in wealth and peace for the rest of their days. They arrogantly refused to accept these offers and ended up either in prison or killed.

Read your history. You will see that nations have been led by men who refused to consider the option of not being in power. Numerous delegations would be sent to advice and even beg a head of state to leave office but he would not. Just like Pharaoh, negotiations and meetings with these stubborn heads of state often fail to have any effect. It is amazing how the pride of Pharaoh has been repeated in the lives of modern day heads of state.

2. **You are puffed up like Pharaoh when you are full of delusions.**

Pharaoh refused to have a new and different relationship with the Israelites. Are you refusing a new relationship that God is bringing your way?

Pharaoh fought against the will of God and kept fighting till the very end. Are you fighting the will of God? Are you still fighting what you should not fight?

Pharaoh had confidence in his armies. Do you have confidence in things that cannot save you?

Pharaoh assumed that he was strong enough to win this battle. Is your pride making you think that you are strong enough to fight even against God?

Pharaoh thought that the victories he had won in the past guaranteed his victory today. Are you relying on the past? Has your pride deluded you?

Pharaoh never admitted that he was wrong. In spite of contrary evidence and in spite of all that had happened he never said he was sorry and he never admitted his mistakes. Is that how you are? If that is how you are, you are just like Pharaoh! You are full of delusions of grandeur! Pride-filled delusions will be your downfall.

3. **We know Pharaoh was puffed up because he fell from his position as the ruler of a powerful country to become the ruler of a destroyed and powerless nation.**

Pharaoh's fall was dramatic and complete in its destruction of Pharaoh. By the time the pride of Pharaoh had run its full course there was no economy, no agriculture and no army in Egypt. He had also lost the nation's building and labour force. He stood in his chariot, staring at the Red Sea as the bodies of his entire army came floating to the shore.

Dear friend, watch out and be careful! Your hardness, your arrogance and your unyieldedness will bring you into a very bad and difficult place. Ask Pharaoh and he will tell you what it is like to lead a nation from the heights of power into the ashes of destruction.

Pharaoh was blinded by his hatred as he pursued the Israelites. The proud king could not believe that anyone could have his way. Arrogant Pharaoh actually believed that he was a god and no one would ever be able to defy him. "And the Egyptians pursued, and went in after them to the midst of the sea, even all Pharaoh's horses, his chariots, and his horsemen.

Those Who Are Proud

And it came to pass, that in the morning watch the Lord looked unto the host of the Egyptians through the pillar of fire and of the cloud, and troubled the host of the Egyptians,

And took off their chariot wheels, that they drave them heavily: so that the Egyptians said, Let us flee from the face of Israel; for the Lord fighteth for them against the Egyptians.

And the Lord said unto Moses, Stretch out thine hand over the sea, that the waters may come again upon the Egyptians, upon their chariots, and upon their horsemen.

And Moses stretched forth his hand over the sea, and the sea returned to his strength when the morning appeared; and the Egyptians fled against it; and the Lord overthrew the Egyptians in the midst of the sea.

And the waters returned, and covered the chariots, and the horsemen, and all the host of Pharaoh that came into the sea after them; THERE REMAINED NOT SO MUCH AS ONE OF THEM" (Exodus 14:23-28).

CHAPTER 16

What It Means To Be Puffed Up Like Korah

Let no one cheat you of your reward, taking delight in false humility and worship of angels, intruding into those things which he has not seen, VAINLY PUFFED UP BY HIS FLESHLY MIND.

Colossians 2:18, NKJV

1. **Korah was puffed up because he thought that the pastor (Moses) was obliged to listen to his opinion.**

   Now Korah, the son of Izhar, the son of Kohath, the son of Levi, and Dathan and Abiram, the sons of Eliab, and On, the son of Peleth, sons of Reuben, took men:

   And they rose up before Moses, with certain of the children of Israel, two hundred and fifty PRINCES OF THE ASSEMBLY, FAMOUS IN THE CONGREGATION, MEN OF RENOWN:

   And they gathered themselves together against Moses and against Aaron, and said unto them, Ye take too much upon you, seeing all the congregation are holy, every one of them, and the Lord is among them: wherefore then lift ye up yourselves above the congregation of the Lord?

   Number 16:1-3

   Korah was a man of repute in society. He thought that because he was a "big man" in society he was also a big man in the church. There are people who feel they must be listened to because of who they are in worldly society.

   Thank God for your banking degree. Thank God for your political achievements! Thank God for your wealth! Thank God that you are now famous! But none of these makes you qualified to tell the pastor what to do. God will lead His servants by His Holy Spirit. The church is led by the Holy Spirit who speaks through His chosen men. The opinions of men, the opinions of lawyers, doctors, administrators, politicians and other men of fame are important. But they do not rule the church! The church is governed by the Holy Spirit who works through His anointed and chosen vessels.

2. **Korah was puffed up because he tried to correct a spiritual authority.**

   ACCUSE NOT A SERVANT UNTO HIS MASTER, lest he curse thee, and thou be found guilty.

   Proverbs 30:10

Spiritual authorities like pastors, priests and bishops are servants of God and their master is Jesus Christ. They are not ordinary people. It is wisdom not to accuse these servants to the Lord. You can easily have a curse coming on your life. Servants of the Lord are called by God, set aside and appointed by the Lord. They are also human beings and do make many mistakes. Any one who says that pastors do not make mistakes does not understand the ministry. Those of us who are ministers are fraught with weaknesses, sins and mistakes. We are actually called and appointed with that in mind. God knows about our weaknesses when He appoints us. Notice this scripture:

> For every high priest taken from among men is appointed on behalf of men in things pertaining to God, in order to offer both gifts and sacrifices for sins; he can deal gently with the ignorant and misguided, SINCE HE HIMSELF ALSO IS BESET WITH WEAKNESS
> Hebrews 5:1-2 (NASB)

As you can see, God knows that pastors and authority figures are beset with weaknesses. This does not give a church member the right or the place to rise up and try to correct them. It is not the place of an ordinary member, no matter how famous or renowned you are, to correct a spiritual authority which God has placed over you.

But that is what Korah tried to do. He was full of himself. He was affected by his fame and renown. He went too far and tried to correct Moses of all people!

God can correct his own authorities and He does. Correcting a spiritual authority is no business of yours even though you may be a long-standing church member.

The sheep cannot lead the shepherd. It is the shepherd who leads the sheep and it is the shepherd who corrects the sheep. Sheep cannot correct the shepherd. God will correct the shepherds Himself.

3. Korah was puffed up because fell from being a man of repute to being wiped out, together with his family.

Korah and his family were wiped out. The earth opened up and Korah and his family disappeared underground. That is what happens to those who step out of order to correct spiritual authorities. Be careful because God will not give up His job of correcting and disciplining His own servants.

Do you want to descend into a pit? Do you want what happened to Korah to happen to you? Then stay in your place! Pray for men of God instead of criticising them. The one who appointed them is the one who can remove them. God does not need your help to point out the failings of His servants. God knew those failings when he was appointing them and yet He called them and sent them to do His will. Moses predicted that people who fought against him would not die an ordinary death. Perhaps today, people die in an unusual way because of things they have said against God's servants.

Notice the words of Moses:

If these men die the common death of all men, or if they be visited after the visitation of all men; then the Lord hath not sent me.

But if the Lord make a new thing, and the earth open her mouth, and swallow them up, with all that appertain unto them, and they go down quick into the pit; then ye shall understand that these men have provoked the LORD.

And it came to pass, as he had made an end of speaking all these words, that the ground clave asunder that was under them:

And the earth opened her mouth, and swallowed them up, and their houses, and all the men that appertained unto Korah, and all their goods.

THEY, AND ALL THAT APPERTAINED TO THEM, WENT DOWN ALIVE INTO THE PIT, and the earth closed upon them: and they perished from among the congregation (Numbers 16:29-33).

CHAPTER 17

What Is It Like To Fall From Pride?

A MAN'S PRIDE SHALL BRING HIM LOW: but honour shall uphold the humble in spirit.

Proverbs 29:23

Pride leads to the destruction of our lives, our businesses and our ministries. "Pride comes before a fall" is one of the commonest statements in our world. Yet we do not really understand what this fall is. The fall and destruction caused by pride takes many different forms. In this chapter, I want you to see the different possible outcomes of pride. All the things in the list below are descriptions of different types of "falls" a person can experience because of pride.

1. **To fall because of pride is to be brought down from your eagle's nest.**

   Thy terribleness hath deceived thee, and the pride of thine heart, O thou that dwellest in the clefts of the rock, that holdest the height of the hill: though THOU SHOULDEST MAKE THY NEST AS HIGH AS THE EAGLE, I WILL BRING THEE DOWN FROM THENCE, saith the Lord.
   Jeremiah 49:16

   A fall from grace is to go from the highest nest of an eagle to the lowest point possible. No matter who you are and no matter how high you have made yourself, pride will bring you down to the lowest place. Mercy upon mercies!

   We need to pray for humility and seek God for the wisdom to walk in humility. Imagine the height of an eagle's nest! How high that is! And yet God can bring you down from there. Oh wow! Ooh!

2. **To fall because of pride is to have your heaven turned into iron and your earth turned into brass.**

   And I will BREAK THE PRIDE of your power; and I WILL MAKE YOUR HEAVEN AS IRON, and your EARTH AS BRASS:
   Leviticus 26:19

   Pride will lead you into spiritual difficulty first of all, in which your heavens will be like iron. Pride will also lead you into difficulties in life because the earth is like brass for a proud person. A fall from grace means that heaven will be difficult to access. Your prayers may no longer be heard because your heaven will be like iron. Life on earth will become even more difficult and complicated because the earth has turned into brass. What a fall! From an open heaven you have fallen to a place where the heavens are closed to you!

3. **To fall because of pride is to be brought down to a place where you do not seek God.**

> The wicked, THROUGH THE PRIDE OF HIS COUNTENANCE, WILL NOT SEEK AFTER GOD: God is not in all his thoughts.
>
> Psalms 10:4

A person who does not seek after God is a fallen human being. When you are normal, you will seek after God and pray to Him. A fall from grace means that you no longer seek after God. You may seek for help from money or other idols. Your pride has brought you down to the place where you worship the gods of silver, gold, wood and stone. What a fall! From worshipping the living God you have fallen to the state of an idol worshipper!

4. **To fall because of pride is to become isolated.**

A fall from grace means that you are cut off. Your tongues, your words and your being are cut off and separated. You will be separated from the Lord and you will also be separated from the people that you need. Proud people are isolated in their castles and have no one to enjoy their lives with. What a fall! From joy, fellowship and constant interaction you have fallen into isolation!

> The Lord shall CUT OFF all flattering lips, and THE TONGUE THAT SPEAKETH PROUD THINGS:
>
> Psalms 12:3

5. **To fall because of pride is to be known from afar.**

> Though the Lord be high, yet hath he respect unto the lowly: but the PROUD HE KNOWETH AFAR OFF.
>
> Psalms 138:6

When you are sent away and made to operate from a distance, you have fallen from the advantageous position of being close. To fall is to be sent away! To fall is to no longer have access! To fall is to be transferred to another department where you never see the boss.

A fall from grace may mean that you can only know God from afar but you cannot come near. When you are important in the government you may be able to go near the presidency and even speak to the president. But when you fall from grace, you can only know the president from afar. You will see him on television, just like everybody else, because you have fallen from grace. What a fall! From closeness you fell into a state of being afar off!

6. To fall because of pride is to be turned into a fool.

God's punishment for your pride is to turn you into a fool. A fall from grace can mean a life of foolishness. God will sentence you to live out the life of a foolish man. Because of your proud statements, angry words and over confident remarks your mind will be darkened and your life will be the life of a fool. What a terrible punishment! What a fall! From wisdom you fell into foolishness!

IN THE MOUTH OF THE FOOLISH IS A ROD OF PRIDE: but the lips of the wise shall preserve them.

Proverbs 14:3

7. To fall because of pride is to enter a world of continuous punishment.

Every one that is proud in heart is an abomination to the Lord: though hand join in hand, HE SHALL NOT BE UNPUNISHED.

Proverbs 16:5

When you fall, you enter the punishment due a proud man. A fall from grace is to enter into a continuous era of punishments. Your whole life is a punishment when you are fallen. What a fall! From a life of freedom and acceptance you now live in a prison you created for yourself.

8. To fall because of pride is to go into captivity.

> But if ye will not hear it, my soul shall weep in secret places for YOUR PRIDE; and mine eye shall weep sore, and run down with tears, because the LORD'S FLOCK IS CARRIED AWAY CAPTIVE.
> Jeremiah 13:17

When you fall into the hands of the devil you go into captivity. A fall from grace means you will be carried away into captivity. This may mean literal captivity such as going to prison. Many proud people are humbled in prison. Many proud people turn to God in prison. This is why the prison ministry is so important. Another form of captivity is spiritual bondage. Spiritual bondage may take the form of demonic oppression. Your pride can lead you into demonic oppression.

9. To fall because of pride is to stumble.

> Behold, I am against thee, O thou most proud, saith the Lord God of hosts: for thy day is come, the time that I will visit thee. And THE MOST PROUD SHALL STUMBLE AND FALL, and none shall raise him up: and I will kindle a fire in his cities, and it shall devour all round about him.
> Jeremiah 50:31-32

A fall from grace is to fall into a state of stumbling. Perhaps God will allow you to stumble through offense. Then all the evils that befall men of bitterness and unforgiveness will descend on you.

You will grope around in uncertainty and confusion as you stumble in the dark. Stumbling in the dark is the state of a fallen human being who has become the enemy of God. God declares that He is against you and will cause you to stumble and fall.

10. To fall because of pride is to enter into depravity.

And even as they did not like to retain God in their knowledge, God gave them over to a reprobate mind, TO DO THOSE THINGS WHICH ARE NOT CONVENIENT;

Being filled with all unrighteousness, fornication, wickedness, covetousness, maliciousness; full of envy, murder, debate, deceit, malignity; whisperers, Backbiters, haters of God, despiteful, PROUD, boasters, inventors of evil things, disobedient to parents, without understanding, covenantbreakers, without natural affection, implacable, unmerciful:

Who knowing the judgment of God, that they which commit such things are worthy of death, not only do the same, but have pleasure in them that do them.

Romans 1:28-32

Proud men who want to have nothing to do with God will fall into depravity. A fall from grace is to fall into depravity. When you are fallen, you are given over to a reprobate mind to do unnatural and depraved things. The unnatural and depraved sexual practices of the western world are a reflection of their pride and subsequent fall from grace.

11. To fall because of pride is to be condemned by the devil.

Not a novice, lest being lifted up with pride he fall into THE CONDEMNATION OF THE DEVIL.

1 Timothy 3:6

A fall from grace is to fall into the condemnation of the devil. When you move away from God, you fall straight into the hands of the devil and into his condemnation. Would you like to fall into the hands of the devil and be under his supervision for eternity in the lake of fire?

A fall from grace is a fall into ignorance, emptiness and delusions. Many proud people are empty barrels making a lot of